FIVE OBSESSIONS OF ELITE ORGANIZATIONS

ADVANCE PRAISE

"Everyone has heard of EOS® and many have used it. If you're ready to go beyond EOS and move up to the next level, read this book…and then get Michael's team involved to help, but only if you're really serious about exponential growth."

—CAMERON HEROLD, Founder of COO Alliance,
author of *Vivid Vision* and *The Second in Command*,
former COO of 1-800-GOT-JUNK?

"I can truly say that the investment we have made with Next Level Growth has been the single most important investment I have ever made in the history of my firm."

—MICHAEL BRADLEY, Founder of Bradley Wealth

"We've worked with Next Level Growth for almost six years and have grown 7x during that time. The investment in the journey is well worth the benefit you will receive if you are ready to take your business to the next level!"

—GRAHAM JOHNSON, CEO of Denova Collaborative Health

"As the CEO, I'm trying to make sure that every dollar we spend is a good investment. Working with Next Level Growth is a no-brainer for us. Every time we meet with our Business Guide, it is money well spent, time well spent, and we're a better company because of it."

—RYAN WOODWARD, CEO of National Technical Institute

"Next Level Growth helped us grow a 100-year-old organization by 91% in our first few years together. Thanks to their guidance, we are a stronger, healthier leadership team that shares the same inspiring purpose and values. I highly recommend a conversation with the Next Level Growth team."

—TIM HEIS, CEO of Goodwill Industries of Dallas

"Our journey with Next Level Growth has been nothing short of extraordinary. Since partnering with them in 2018, our company, Embark Behavioral Health— one of the country's leading youth mental health providers—has been able to scale the number of families we have served by 5x in just five years. I whole-heartedly recommend Next Level Growth to any organization seeking to build a tighter leadership team, increase accountability and clarity, unlock their full potential, and achieve extraordinary results."

—ALEX STAVROS, Former CEO of Embark Behavioral Health

"Love the entire team at Next Level Growth! I've worked with a lot of coaches and systems for entrepreneurial organizations, and Next Level Growth is exactly that: Next Level. Their organization, thoughtfulness, customization, and partner-ship are invaluable to any growth-oriented company. Whether you're a low- or high-functioning team, your company will definitely see the ROI when working with this group."

—ALEX TAYLOR, Partner and COO of 34th Floor Hospitality

"We've experienced a tremendous amount of professional and personal growth through working with the team at Next Level Growth, and our business is so much better now than it ever has been. Personally, the biggest benefit to me as the CEO of Sensei has been to be able to focus on my passions and enable others to do the same with clear ownership and expectations for every role. The entire team and Next Level Growth is awesome, and they enjoy having fun in the process."

—KENNETH STEINESS, CEO of Sensei Project Solutions

FIVE

OBSESSIONS

— OF —

ELITE

ORGANIZATIONS

Take Your Business and Your Life to the Next Level

MICHAEL ERATH

LIONCREST

PUBLISHING

FIRST EDITION

FIVE OBSESSIONS OF ELITE ORGANIZATIONS
Take Your Business and Your Life to the Next Level

ISBN 978-1-5445-4785-5 *Hardcover*
        978-1-5445-4784-8 *Paperback*
        978-1-5445-4786-2 *Ebook*

This book is dedicated to my wife, Elizabeth,
for encouraging me to transition to a new career path as
a Business Guide in 2015 and her unwavering support
along the way. It is also dedicated to our incredible team of
Partners and Business Guides at Next Level Growth for
all we do to sharpen each other as we continue
to learn, grow, and evolve together.

"The only thing standing between you and what you want, is you and what you are not willing to do."

—LARRY WINGET

CONTENTS

Chapter 1

WHY DO I NEED A BUSINESS OPERATING SYSTEM?

"Every system is perfectly designed
to get the results it gets."

—PAUL BATALDEN

Whether you're an owner, leader, or manager of an entrepreneurial organization, imagine, for a moment, your organization two years from today. What date will that be? I want to challenge you to write that date in the front of this book and even mark it on your calendar with the heading "Five Obsessions of Elite Organizations" and "Return on Life."

Imagine it is now that day, just two years from now. Everyone from the CEO to the front lines is crystal clear on what is expected of them in their roles, both in terms of cultural alignment and performance. They are all part of a process that maintains alignment, with outstanding communication between every leader and the people in their charge. There is active coaching when someone is underperforming, and leadership, as well as the entire organization, supports team members being coached. At the same time, underperformers who are not successful at being coached up are being coached out.

Team members are also aligned and inspired by the purpose and values of the organization. They understand the behaviors and actions expected of them in order to fit the culture. They know how to explain to family and friends what the organization really stands for and how what they do is meaningful work.

Everyone has been well trained and has checklists and playbooks to serve as reminders of how work flows in the organization, so there is consistency from team to team, and errors and mistakes are kept to a minimum. When team members find a gap, or waste, in their processes, they collaborate to make and communicate improvements, constantly making their work more efficient and effective.

People know how they are being measured, how they contribute to the success of the organization, and that their wins are being consistently celebrated. They are being coached and developed within a high-performing culture that equips them for success, and those who want to grow in their career have a clear path available to them. Leaders and managers are focused on building relationships with the people they lead, and as a result, team members feel that their voices are being heard. They feel supported and confident that their leaders have their backs and will rush to help them when they need it.

Across the entire organization, people understand how their role contributes to the financial health of the organization and why it matters. Leaders invest time in teaching financial literacy at all levels and help team members connect the dots between the importance of profit and cash flow in supporting payroll, performance bonuses, and strong benefits. They help them understand how a focus on growing profits and cash flow leads to more reinvestment into the business to make conditions better and make jobs easier to perform through better tools, equipment, software, and more.

How much better will your organization operate when all of these things are true? How much more profitable will the organization be as a result of gained efficiency, reduced errors and mistakes, and lower turnover? How much more resilient to a downturn will your organization be, allowing it to avoid layoffs and downsizing in a weak economy? How much easier will it be for you to grow? How much more satisfied will your customers be as a result of the increased consistency of your products or services? How much more enjoyable will your own job be as a leader or manager when your team members "get it" and when they are aligned and clear, working together and communicating well?

Those are the realities of an elite organization. For you, it means more than a Return on Investment for the time and energy you pour into your work; it means you are earning a meaningful *Return on Life*.

Whether you realize it or not, your business already has its own aggregation of "operating systems." In most cases, it is by default, having organically taken shape as the business has grown. In other instances, it has come about by intentional, well-thought-out design. In far too many cases, it is the former. And unfortunately, that is the cause of many of the struggles organizations face.

The truth is, if your business is not growing as fast as you want it to, your business has a system designed to grow at a slower rate than you would like.

If your business is not as profitable as you would like, your business has a system designed to generate a lower profit than you would like.

If you struggle to find and keep good employees and your people are driving you nuts, then your business has a system designed to find and retain people who are not of the caliber you need, and therefore, they drive you nuts.

If you struggle with customer or client attrition due to inconsistencies with your products or services, your business has a system designed to produce inconsistent outcomes that drive away your customers or clients.

If you want a better result, you need a better system.

When you follow the Five Obsessions framework, what you will get as a by-product is a custom-tailored business operating system that puts you and your organization, not the system, first. It will significantly increase clarity and alignment throughout the organization, leading to greater communication and collaboration within teams as well as between teams. This will result in more consistency. It will lead to a better employee experience. That will improve retention and reduce turnover. With greater consistency and happier employees who stay, you will get a more satisfying customer or client experience that will bring down client attrition and allow you to grow your business with your existing clients. You will create internal and external raving fans who are ambassadors of your business and your services or products.

More than that, you will have a business that accomplishes two extraordinary things. First, you will be able to maximize the ROI (Return on Investment) from your business. If you are the owner, this will happen through growth in the overall value of the business, whether your intention is to keep it and pass it on or to eventually exit the business through a liquidity event. If you are a leader or manager, your maximum ROI will come from an organization capable of compensating its high achievers at above-industry pay rates, with merit-based incentives allowing you to earn more for yourself and your family than you could anywhere else.

In addition, when you successfully execute each of the Five Obsessions, you will also be able to maximize what we call a *Return on Life*. You will have highly capable, aligned teams who are executing their missions consistently and effectively, freeing you from the typical firefighting and frustrations that consume leaders in mediocre organizations. That freedom will allow you to have more time for thinking bigger and being more strategic, while also giving you time back. Time is a priceless, finite resource that needs to be protected so you can spend sufficient amounts of it with family, friends, relationships, and most importantly, tending to your own physical and emotional health and well being. Every day you spend frustrated and burned out is a day you are sacrificing and will never get back. If you follow what you will find in these pages, in time, those days of high stress, anxiety, and frustration will become few and far between.

In this book, I will also make clear what employees gain when their organizations adopt the Five Obsessions with fanatical consistency. After all, they are the ones on the front lines making things happen, and their buy-in to the principles is critical in the successful adoption of this framework.

In his popular and well-respected book, *The Great Game of Business*, Jack Stack writes:

> The only way to be secure [in business] is to make money and generate cash. Everything else is a means to that end... And yet, at most companies, people are never told that the survival of the company depends on those two things. People are told what to do in an eight-hour workday, but no one ever shows them how they fit into a bigger picture. No one explains how one person's actions affect another person's actions, how

each department depends on the others, or what impact they all have on the company as a whole. Most importantly, no one tells people how they make money and generate cash. Nine times out of ten, employees don't even know the difference between the two.[1]

This book will give you everything you need to solve that puzzle.

In these pages, you will find a roadmap, not just of theoretical ideas, but of highly practical tools and concepts, with real-world examples to follow, that you can begin to use to get better results on your way to building elite teams and an elite organization. You will be given specific instructions on how to use the tools and how to customize them to your organization. In addition, you will get real-world examples from companies working with Next Level Growth Business Guides highlighting what things were like before using a specific tool or concept, how they went about implementing and utilizing it, what challenges they faced along the way, how they overcame those challenges, and what the outcome was after the successful deployment of the tool or concept.

The principles you will learn about in this book are also time-tested and proven. Successful organizations have been using them for hundreds of years and will be using them for hundreds more. And not just the big, well-known, successful corporations. Consider my alma mater, High Point University (HPU), a highly successful organization that accomplished an extraordinary transformation of its own.

In 1991, I was a college freshman, and that year, High Point College became High Point University. Enrollment was barely more than 1,000 students. In 2005, just ten years after I graduated, Dr. Nido Qubein took over as president of the university, marking the first time an entrepreneur had been placed at the helm of the organization, which had

---

1 Jack Stack, *The Great Game of Business: The Only Sensible Way to Run a Company* (Crown Business, 2013), 35.

historically been led by Methodist ministers with backgrounds in academia. He inherited a campus of old buildings resting on ninety-one acres, with declining enrollment of 1,450 students and $120 million in deferred maintenance costs. In Nido's own words, "The institution was living on borrowed time...staring in the face of all that deferred maintenance scared me half to death."[2]

From 2005 through 2025, 108 new buildings have been built or acquired on the campus, which has expanded from ninety-one to more than 550 acres. Ten new academic schools have been founded, nearly three billion dollars have been invested, and for eleven straight years, *US News & World Report* has ranked High Point University number one on the list of best colleges in the South. Under Dr. Qubein's leadership, it truly has become an elite organization.

The youngest of five children, Nido Qubein lost his father to illness when he was six years old. This left his mother, a seamstress with a fourth-grade education, to work day and night to feed and clothe her children amidst ongoing civil unrest in Lebanon. They lived very modestly, but she was loving and wise and often told her children that "poverty was only temporary" and "you may be poor in your pocket, but you can always be wealthy in your heart."

His mother held on to the dream that her children would go to college, and she was determined that her youngest son would be educated in America. At the age of seventeen, with very little knowledge of the English language, Nido left the Middle East behind and boarded a one-way flight to the United States. He had only fifty dollars in his pocket.

Nido chose to attend Mount Olive College (now University of Mount Olive) in North Carolina because the name reminded him of Jerusalem's

---

2 Nido Qubein, *Extraordinary Transformation* (High Point University, 2024), 3.

Mount of Olives. To make ends meet, he worked as a public relations director at a local YMCA and in work-study programs in the school's cafeteria and library. Nido had a charming personality and a love for people and building relationships, which led to an uncanny ability to connect with others. At the end of his second year, he learned that an anonymous donor had paid for the gap between his payments to the college and the cost of his tuition. On that day, Nido vowed to someday find a way to help other young people in need get a college education.

He completed his undergraduate education at High Point College while working as a church youth leader, growing the group's enrollment from fifteen to 150. Motivated by what he saw as a lack of curriculum for youth in the church, while still in graduate school at the University of North Carolina—Greensboro, he started a newsletter called "Adventures with Youth" for churches, camps, and schools. It provided content for activities and programs to help youth grow and develop leadership skills. Through tireless marketing and outreach, he grew his newsletter's audience from 1,000 in the first year to 68,000 subscribers in thirty-two countries at its peak.

His ability to grow enterprises by leaps and bounds continued when, after receiving his MBA in the 1970s, he became a public speaker with hundreds of annual engagements, owner of a business development leadership consulting and publications firm, and author of over a dozen books. In 2001, he took over as chairman of the world's first whole wheat bakery franchise, Great Harvest Bread Company, while also serving on the board of his alma mater, High Point University.

After several years on the board of HPU, he was stunned when he was invited to take over as president of the university and even more taken aback when he realized how deficient it was in resources. His commitment to helping young people in need pursue their education never wavered, however, so he took on the challenge in 2005. Driven by this inspiring purpose, he embarked on his greatest journey yet of extraordinary, exponential growth, determined to embody his mother's words that "Poverty is only temporary."

While not specifically using Next Level Growth's *Five Obsessions of Elite Organizations* as his framework, the transformative journey Dr. Nido Qubein led the organization through and wrote about in his 2024 book, *Extraordinary Transformation*, followed a parallel path and, on reflection, leveraged the same five principles that are at the core of the Five Obsessions. I chose to share his story and his reflections on his tenure at High Point University from a conversation we had leading up to the writing of this book to highlight the time-tested nature of these five principles. At the time this book was published, Nido had just celebrated his twentieth year at the helm of what has become known as the "premier life-skills university of the South." I would encourage you to read his book and learn from his profound leadership and accomplishments at High Point University. It is an extraordinary example of the possibilities your own elite organization will have when you embrace these principles and adopt the Next Level Growth framework, Five Obsessions of Elite Organizations®.

> "I'm incredibly proud of High Point University. For 20 years,
> we've grown every year in every aspect and every metric.
> In retention, enrollment, financial performance, and rankings.
> That's the way leadership should be. And that's the way an enterprise
> should be. They should always shoot for better tomorrows.
> The tomorrows of your life should be better than the yesterdays
> of your life. The more you do that, the better off you are."[3]
>
> —DR. NIDO QUBEIN

---

3 Nido Qubein, interview by the author, October 14, 2024.

WHY LISTEN TO ME?

It is very likely that you and I have never met, and as such, I don't pretend to know your specific circumstances, your opportunities, challenges, frustrations, or your dreams for your life and how your career plays a role in those dreams. But after thirty years as an entrepreneur and business owner, as someone who has grown a business to forty-five million dollars in revenue, with over 200 employees and offices on six continents, as someone who lost it all to an unscrupulous business partner convicted of embezzlement and bank fraud, as someone who picked up the pieces of a shattered life, started over from nothing, and went on to build a second business to seven million dollars before transitioning to a Business Guide as Founder of Next Level Growth, I believe I've come to know more than just a few things about what works and what does not. I've learned the hard way about the sacrifices that leaders make and the things we trade off in order to grow our organizations and our careers.

Now that I am ten years into the second half of my career, together with a team of elite Partners and Business Guides at Next Level Growth, I have discovered, and we have collectively refined, a principled approach to building elite organizations. I am choosing to write this book to take what the first half of my life has taught me and share it openly with anyone who is willing to listen and learn. In the process, I hope to pay it forward and maybe, just maybe, save you from possibly experiencing the great loss that once happened to me by building an elite organization focused on these five timeless principles.

WHAT THIS BOOK IS, AND WHAT IT IS NOT

In recent years, it has become very common that, as part of a marketing strategy, many business coaches and consultants are encouraged to write a book. The majority of those books are often little more than a rewrite or reframing of more popular existing books by very well-known thought leaders, and as a result, most of them fail to give the reader much content that is new and valuable to be able to start using. There is often little that will add immediate positive impact to the work that they do. This is something I was very well aware of and sensitive to when I set out to write *Five Obsessions of Elite Organizations*.

This book is different. It is about the latest evolution in thought around operating an entrepreneurial organization. It is based foundationally on a principled approach rather than the more common prescriptive systems that have become very popular and very commonplace since the early 2000s. The principled approach you will learn about in this book is about freedom. It is about outcomes and results, with a focus on customization as needed. It is about the user first, not the system first. It starts with a vision of a destination—an overarching long-term objective for the organization. Then, based on a relentless focus on five specific principles, which we call obsessions, it requires the building of a framework of internal systems, leveraging tools and concepts specifically sourced and designed to be custom-fitted to your organization.

If one of the recommended tools to reach an objective doesn't feel right to your organization or team, a principled approach gives you the freedom to select a different tool that will accomplish the same objective so that you can find the right tools, applied in the right ways, to suit your unique culture, industry, and circumstances. A principled approach puts primacy on you, the user, not the system.

WHO THIS BOOK IS FOR

This book is for anyone who wants to build an elite organization or an elite team within an organization. The principles at the core of this book apply whether your organization is a for-profit or a nonprofit, and it will add significant value in either case. If you're a founding entrepreneur, this book is for you. If you're a CEO or president, this book is for you. If you're a member of an executive team, this book is for you. If you're a vice president or a manager of a function within an organization, this book is for you. If you're a supervisor leading a front-line team, this book is for you.

But first, I want to clarify how I define an "elite" organization. *Merriam-Webster* defines the term "elite" when used as an adjective: "Superior in quality, rank, skill, etc." While I believe that the general definition holds true, I also think that every leader, whether of an organization or a team within an organization, needs to understand their own personal definition of the term.

For some, an elite organization might be the leading innovator in their industry. For others, it might be the biggest, the most profitable, or the fastest growing. For others, it might be slightly different. For some, an elite organization is one that is self-managing and led by a team of outstanding people so that the founder is able to spend time doing things that bring them joy in life. For others, perhaps those who are leaders and managers of teams in organizations, it may be that their teams are high-performing, well-trained, and highly collaborative so that they can be free from the constant firefighting and distractions that come from leading mediocre or misaligned teams.

Everyone will have their own definition of what an elite organization looks like to them. No one definition can apply to everyone. At the same time, not everyone will have the willingness or interest in the consistent commitment to extreme discipline to build something that can truly be considered elite.

I specifically chose the word obsession in our branding because when you study the leaders who have truly built something elite, you will find that their commitment, drive, and passion around these principles was to a level that can only be described as an obsession.

When you get clear about what you need in order to get more than just a Return on Investment from your business or career and to actually earn a meaningful *Return on Life*, you will begin to bring into focus what "elite" looks like for you and the team or teams you lead.

Whether your definition has you grinding it out at the helm for your entire career or leads to a place of entrepreneurial freedom that allows you time and space to enjoy the fruits of your labor, you will have to embrace and excel at a core set of principles, what we call the Five Obsessions of Elite Organizations, in order to truly achieve greatness.

When we talk about leaders and elite organizations, many sports fans may think about Phil Jackson, who won eleven NBA championships as the head coach of two different organizations, six with the Chicago Bulls and five with the LA Lakers. Clearly, there was something special about Phil Jackson's approach that led to such incredible success. Yes, he had Jordan, Pippen, and Rodman in Chicago and Kobe and Shaq in LA, but those players also played for other coaches and did not have the same level of success, so there must be clues in Phil Jackson's story as to what it takes to build something elite.

Others may think of businesses like Apple under Steve Jobs and Steve Wozniak, or SpaceX, or other high-growth companies that are on the leading edge of technological innovation. In my own research over the years, one thing has become increasingly clear: the best of the best organizations, in one way or another, are obsessed with their focus on a handful of common principles and then with building systems and executing those systems to a very high level, in order to achieve extraordinary outcomes relative to the handful of principles on which they are focused.

The principles are the foundation of the Five Obsessions of Elite Organizations and hold the keys to escaping a sea of mediocrity and moving into a blue ocean, where the best of the best organizations become a category of one in their space. Even if your vision is not to embrace the level of discipline that the world would see as elite, better is still better, and using what is in these pages will lead to better outcomes for you and the teams or organizations you lead.

If your organization has already been using a business operating system like EOS®, Scaling Up®, or others, and you either quit because it didn't feel right for your organization or you lost the discipline and focus to maintain it and you've slipped back into old habits, or even if you truly mastered it and are just wondering, "What's next?" this book is for you. In fact, nearly 80 percent of our clients left another business operating system to work with Next Level Growth and learn the Five Obsessions of Elite Organizations, which is further evidence that in the pages of this book, if you're already using a business operating system, you will find a better way.

With full transparency, I will always believe that when it comes to your time, priorities, and proficiency, your organization is always better off working with a Next Level Growth Partner and Business Guide to increase the velocity of your acceleration and growth as you transition to the Five Obsessions framework. However, I do recognize as someone who is a confessed "self-implementer" of EOS® (the Entrepreneurial Operating System® made popular in the 2007 book *Traction* by Gino Wickman) that for many smaller organizations, it is often a matter of affordability. Others simply prefer taking a do-it-yourself approach. After using Wickman's *Traction* system in a former business I started in 2010 and making the Inc. 5000 in 2015, I can personally attest that taking the do-it-yourself approach can still be effective. Because I believe so strongly in the value of what we have created in the Five Obsessions, I want to give you the do-it-yourself foundation for only the cost of this book, with the hope that, in time, it will eventually bring some of you back to one of our Expert Guides at Next Level Growth.

If you do chose to follow the do-it-yourself approach, to help you, I have been hard at work creating a clone of myself, available at **AskMichaelErath.com**, that you can use for a nominal cost to get questions answered and assistance from me along your path to self-implementation.

WHAT IS POSSIBLE IF YOU STUDY AND USE THIS BOOK AS YOUR FIELD GUIDE

Jim Collins opens his 2001 best-selling book *Good to Great* by stating that "Good is the enemy of great." Having spent more than twenty years growing my own businesses, followed by more than 10,000 hours across well over 1,000 days personally guiding strategic meetings with the leadership teams of more than 100 entrepreneurial organizations, I could not agree more.

If you commit to studying, learning, and leveraging *with fanatical consistency* the framework you will learn in this book, you will not only move your organization closer to greatness, but you will also begin to experience greater freedom and joy. This kind of freedom and joy comes only to those who are willing to bring a special discipline, commitment, passion, and drive to excel. You will learn to do this by building the future of your organization around *Great People*, aligned and driven by an *Inspiring Purpose*, consistently training on, executing, and continuously improving *Optimized Playbooks*, in a *Culture of Performance*, while proactively *Growing Profits and Cash Flow*.

These are the Five Obsessions of Elite Organizations, and they hold the keys to unlocking a future of unimaginable potential for those courageous enough to make the disciplined and often difficult decisions required to build something elite...elevating your organization to a category of one in your market.

To fully understand this new and evolved approach, how and why it is different from anything that has come before, and what that means for you, it is important to first understand how we got here. It is necessary to understand the evolution of business operating systems.

Chapter 2

THE EVOLUTION OF BUSINESS OPERATING SYSTEMS

"It's dangerous not to evolve."

—JEFF BEZOS

Figure 2.1

Over the first two decades of the twenty-first century, the concept of entrepreneurs "systemizing" their businesses and using a "business operating system" became exponentially more mainstream and attainable. In general, regardless of the system used, an intentionally systemized business almost always consistently outperforms any competitors who lack an intentionally organized system on which to operate the business as a whole.

Whether you are already using one or you've never heard of the concept, to understand and confirm which system is optimal for you and your organization, it is important to understand the evolution of business operating systems. This chapter will take you back to the early beginnings and help you understand how these systems evolved, what key differences exist between the more popular ones, and highlight the differences between a *prescriptive system* and a *principled approach*.

WHAT IS A BUSINESS OPERATING SYSTEM?

A business operating system is basically an organized set of processes through which a business manages strategy development and execution to guide the energy and focus of people within the organization and achieve common goals as it grows.

Two of the more well-known systems in the market over the last two decades have been Scaling Up and EOS. Both systems are based on similar fundamentals and are generally prescriptive and static. More on this later.

The Evolution of Business Operating Systems— A Brief Overview

While the concept of systemizing a business has its roots as far back as the Industrial Revolution, it started to become more popular and formalized in the early 1900s. One key figure in this development was W. Edwards Deming, an American engineer, statistician, professor, author, lecturer, and management consultant. Deming is widely credited with helping to launch the quality revolution in Japan after World War II through his work on statistical process control and his popular *14 Points for Management.*

For those of you who appreciate history, other early thought leaders in the field of systemizing businesses were:

- **Frederick Winslow Taylor:** Known for his work on scientific management, Taylor's ideas emphasized the scientific study of work methods to improve productivity. His book *The Principles of Scientific Management* (1911) is a seminal work in this field.
- **Henry Ford:** Ford was president of Ford Motor Company from 1906 to 1919. While primarily known for revolutionizing the automobile industry with his assembly line techniques, Ford's ideas also had a significant impact on the concept of systemizing business operations.
- **Peter Drucker:** Drucker was a management consultant, educator, and author, often referred to as the "founder of modern management." His book *The Practice of Management* (1954) is a classic in the field and covers various aspects of managing organizations, including the importance of systematic approaches.
- **W. Edwards Deming:** Deming, as mentioned earlier, was a key figure in the quality revolution in Japan. His book *Out*

of the Crisis (1982) outlines his management philosophy and principles, which emphasize the importance of quality and continual improvement in business processes.

- **Eliyahu M. Goldratt:** Goldratt's book *The Goal: A Process of Ongoing Improvement* (1984) introduced the Theory of Constraints, which focuses on identifying and improving the constraints that limit a system's performance, leading to more effective systemization.
- **Michael Gerber:** Gerber is best known for his book *The E-Myth Revisited: Why Most Small Businesses Don't Work and What to Do About It* (originally published in 1985), which emphasizes the importance of systemizing and standardizing business processes to achieve success and scalability.
- **Jack Stack:** In his 1992 classic, *The Great Game of Business*, which introduced the concept of open-book management, Stack lays out the process for how he and twelve other employees from International Harvester purchased a part of the company that remanufactured truck engines and took it from sixteen million dollars in annual revenue to over one billion over a twenty-five-year period.

Until Gerber released *The E-Myth*, most of the research and writings on systemizing businesses were focused on the operational aspects of the business, and especially on manufacturing. Gerber was among the first to focus on the organization as a whole and apply the idea of systemization to its entirety.

Gerber's book addressed the common dilemma facing most entrepreneurs, that of being stuck as technicians in their own businesses. Many entrepreneurs simply don't understand how to systemize things through the creation and delegation of clearly defined processes to get out of their own way and scale their business.

THE E-MYTH IN REALITY

One example of this "e-myth" evolution is commonly found in the home services industry. Many of the companies in this space that we have helped to scale have been started by a founder who was working as a technician in someone else's business.

Jerry grew up in the commercial construction industry and worked his way up to being a project manager in a large general contracting firm in Phoenix. Over time, Jerry grew dissatisfied with the culture, especially with his boss, and decided that he would start his own construction company. In doing so, he wanted to build something with a fun and engaging culture so people wouldn't have to work in the kind of environment he had for so many years.

In the beginning, Jerry was the one doing business development and meeting with potential clients. They loved the chance to work with him because they were dealing directly with the owner, and his enthusiasm was infectious. When it was time to submit bids, it was Jerry who was putting together and delivering the proposals. Since he was the owner, he was able to work through negotiations fast, making key decisions on the spot, with no need to go back to anybody for approval, and as a result, he was able to win work over his bigger, slower, more corporate competitors with ease.

When it came time to start the projects, Jerry was also the project manager, and oftentimes even filled the role of supervisor, which would put him physically on-site during much of the time the project was underway. Again, that personal involvement and oversight were appreciated by his clients, and he continued to grow and win work.

As Jerry got busier and more and more opportunities came in, he began having a hard time keeping up with the bids and proposals he needed to be working on while at the same time overseeing the work in the field, not to mention keeping up with the banking and bookkeeping. Early mornings, long days, and late nights became the norm. Jerry had trouble making time for his friendships and recreational activities. He was too busy to spend the time he wanted to with his family. His physical health began to suffer, and over time, his emotional health began to suffer as well.

Slowly, cracks began to form in the business, and eventually, things began to break.

Jerry's business had outgrown his ability to be the "jack of all trades" and keep all the balls in the air at the same time. He had to start recruiting and hiring people to come in and help him, and it wasn't just other technical trades roles he needed help with. While he did need to bring in a project manager and a few supervisors to help with job oversight and estimating for proposals, he also needed to bring in a bookkeeper to help him keep up with all the accounting and banking tasks. Eventually, Jerry would even need to bring in someone to help him with his business development efforts as well.

But what if the supervisors and project managers don't do things the way I like to see them done? he would worry to himself. *If I give up control of that part of the business, I might lose some of the relationships that I've worked so hard to build.*

Jerry had become the e-myth. He had started the business with a passion and excitement that was visible to everyone around him. But over time, the business had become a burden, one that would suck much of the joy out of his life.

Jerry's thoughts and concerns were no different than many founders at this stage, and like most, he got stuck worrying about it and didn't know what to do. As a result, he began to micromanage new hires rather than provide them with the proper training and documentation needed to establish clear expectations around things like client experience and quality standards for work.

This was the tipping point for Jerry, just like it is for so many founders as they grow their businesses. They've never had to recruit and interview for positions that are outside their area of expertise. They've never had to delegate tasks to other people. They've never had to trust and hope that those people will handle the tasks the same way that they would. They've never had to build out documented processes and manage the training of new team members. They've never had to onboard new employees or manage expenses and overheads in a growing business.

As a result, many businesses stagnate at that early stage and never move beyond the founder as the key employee doing most of the work. In other cases, founders lose control with a mix of misaligned new hires all going in different directions, completely changing the culture and the client experience for the worse, and the business ultimately fails.

Jerry's story is exactly what Gerber wrote about in *The E-Myth*, but fortunately, Jerry was able to keep things together until he eventually found his way to a Next Level Growth Partner and Business Guide. Today, his business is thriving under the leadership of a strong and aligned team, allowing Jerry to take more time for himself to invest in friendships, relationships, and recurring Fridays on the golf course with a few of his closest friends.

MASTERING THE ROCKEFELLER HABITS

In 1991, just a few years following his founding of YEO (Young Entrepreneurs' Organization—now known as EO or Entrepreneurs'

Organization), Verne Harnish created the Birthing of Giants program in partnership with MIT and *Inc.* magazine.[4] For the next ten years, Harnish committed his time and energy to exploring and developing the foundational ideas known as the "Rockefeller Habits."

In 2002, Harnish published the book *Mastering the Rockefeller Habits*. Two years later, shortly after the passing of my father, I joined the Young Presidents' Organization's (YPO) Southern Seven Chapter as president and CEO of our hardwood veneer manufacturing business, Erath Veneer. Together with my Forum Group, we studied and implemented many of the tools and concepts from Verne's book.

After reading *Mastering the Rockefeller Habits*, I implemented Daily Huddles at Erath Veneer throughout various teams in our organization. As an executive team, we started following the Weekly Meeting Agenda from the book. We also began to gain clarity on our data and how to report the right numbers to the right people to drive performance. All of it was helpful, and it was this book that sparked a passion in me for learning and understanding the science behind how great businesses work.

I was thirty-three years old at that time, and while the book contained a valuable set of tools and concepts, they had not yet fully evolved into a holistic system, as they later would be when Harnish published *Scaling Up, Mastering the Rockefeller Habits 2.0*.

During the late 1990s, according to an article written by Verne Harnish, one of the founding members of the Detroit Chapter of YEO, Gino Wickman, was also using the Rockefeller Habits tools and techniques to turn around and eventually exit his family business. According to

---

4 Verne Harnish, "Are You Considering Implementing Scaling Up or EOS in Your Business? Not Sure Which Is Right for You?," Scaling Up: A Gazelles Company, accessed December 5, 2024, https://scalingup.com/scalingup-vs-eos-comparing-systems-implementation-costs/.

Harnish, "[Gino] later became one of our early coaching partners when we started [Gazelles]. He specifically represented and exclusively used the Rockefeller Habits to coach other companies on behalf of my firm—and was an outstanding coach for us."[5]

As often happens in the entrepreneurial world, and as Gerber wrote about in *The E-Myth*, a person works for an organization, learns a set of skills, and in doing so comes up with either a better way to do things or a way to solve problems they see as not being solved with the existing product. The courageous ones often go off to start their own business to make those improvements and take them to market. This is what Jerry did in starting his own construction business; it is what Gino Wickman did sometime around the turn of the century, and it is what I would do with two close friends and important colleagues, Greg Cleary and Duane Marshall, some twenty years later.

Figure 2.2
L to R: Duane Marshall, Michael Erath, and Greg Cleary shortly after
the creation of Pinnacle Business Guides and Next Level Growth.

5 Harnish, "Are You Considering Implementing Scaling Up or EOS in Your Business?"

TRACTION

According to Wickman's LinkedIn profile and the history of EOS from the company's website, it was in September of 2000, after leaving Verne Harnish and Gazelles, that Wickman took what he had learned and experienced to that point and began evolving and creating what eventually became EOS, the Entrepreneurial Operating System. In 2007, Wickman published the book *Traction*, a very impactful book that has been embraced by entrepreneurs around the world.

The following year, in 2008, Wickman officially launched EOS Worldwide® with a team of eight EOS Implementers®. From that original group, the organization has now scaled to nearly one thousand EOS Implementers around the world. It has also been purchased by a private equity firm and continues to expand with more coaches in more countries.

In 2011, after transitioning from YPO to EO, again with a Forum Group I was in, we read and worked together to self-implement *Traction* in our own businesses. For me, this was a more applicable solution than the original *Mastering the Rockefeller Habits* because the system was holistic, and there was a simple-to-follow path to implement the tools.

While I received tremendous value out of reading and implementing the tools and concepts in *Traction*, based on my prior experiences as an entrepreneur, there were some parts of EOS where I felt certain tools were not ideal for my organization or culture. Take, for example, their People Analyzer™, which I felt failed to provide the level of clarity and specificity I wanted when it came to identifying A-Players relative to B- and C-Players. In other cases, during the course of my career and time in YPO, I felt that I had found a different tool, from a different system or thought leader, that would accomplish the same outcome but in an even better and more impactful way. As a result, I substituted some of the EOS tools in favor of other tools and concepts that I felt were better suited for my organization and would lead to better results. In some cases, I even created and added my own tools rooted in concepts from thought leaders like Jim Collins, Simon Sinek, Ken Iverson, and others, which I felt filled in some gaps that I found to exist within EOS.

EVOLVING FROM EOS—PART ONE

During my time as CEO of Erath Veneer, long before *Traction* was published, and from my study of *Mastering the Rockefeller Habits*, I was fascinated by the Profit per X concept that Jim Collins discusses in his 2001 book, *Good to Great*. In that book, Collins writes, "The Good-to-Great companies frequently produced spectacular returns in very unspectacular industries. Each of them gained profound insights into their economics and, as a result, built a fabulous economic engine."[6] That concept, of building a *fabulous economic engine*, became a passion of mine. We studied it from every angle and analyzed our business through the lens of discovering our Profit per X to build our fabulous economic engine, and after several months, with the help of my CFO Bob Moore, we found it.

There were two keys to helping us arrive at our Profit per X. First, as a manufacturing business where adding a new production line to expand capacity would have required an investment of around five million dollars, it was cost-prohibitive to just expand capacity to grow profits. We had to figure out how to become more profitable through the constraints of our existing capacity. It was becoming clear to us that

---

6 Jim Collins, *Good to Great: Why Some Companies Make the Leap…and Others Don't* (Harper Business, 2001), 104.

our Profit per X should have something to do with throughput, which we measured in board feet (board feet is a standard unit of measure in the hardwood industry).

At the same time, we only had a few lines of variable operating expenses in our financials. The majority of our expenses and overheads were either entirely or predominately fixed costs. This allowed us to have a clear understanding, within about a 5 percent variance, of what we needed to generate in monthly Gross Profit dollars to cover expenses and overheads and make our first dollar of operating profit.

As those two things became clear to us, we had a breakthrough. If we could measure, analyze, and consistently improve our Gross Profit Dollars per Board Foot Produced, we could build a fabulous economic engine. While this is not the place to go too far into the details (I will do that in Chapter 7), we used a standard manufacturing cost system and had standard prices in the system for every specie and every grade (think of those as our SKUs) built into our ERP (Enterprise Resource Planning) system. This allowed us to predict the future Gross Profit dollars that would come from everything we produced. A decade later, when I became an EOS Implementer myself, Profit per X became one of many *"Beyond EOS"* tools I taught and helped my clients use to build their own fabulous economic engines.

Armed with our new Profit per X, we began to analyze everything: vendors, buyers, product lines, customers, salespeople…everything was analyzed in terms of contribution to our Profit per X. Anything that was underperforming was either improved or removed. In just eighteen months of obsessive analysis and implementation of improvements to drive our Profit per X, we were able to generate an average of $100,000 of additional Gross Profit every month, and we did that without spending additional operating expense dollars to get the profit, which meant nearly all of it found its way to the bottom line.

EVOLVING FROM EOS—PART 2

From that time on, I continued to focus on the idea of building a fabulous economic engine. That continued focus led to the creation of what we now teach and refer to as a *Most Critical Outcome*® or *MCO*®.

One frustration I had when I was self-implementing EOS in my next business, North American Veneer, was with the second bullet point under the Data Component™, what they call "Measurables for All." The concept is that everyone in the organization has a number that defines success for them in their role. The problem I encountered is that while the book gives you eight good reasons that everyone should have a number, it doesn't give you any insights into how you can figure out what that should be, so it ends up as more of a theoretical concept than a tactical item. In fact, at Next Level Growth, we have yet to onboard a new client who has come over from EOS and has solved the puzzle to establish "Measurables for All," something we have solved for and now teach all of our clients from the very beginning of our work with them.

Using our Profit per X to make business decisions helped us begin to look at everything through the lens of ROI—Return on Investment. That mindset led me to a breakthrough that eventually framed the concept of a Most Critical Outcome after I transitioned to a professional services business and started Next Level Growth. What I realized was that in my professional services business, as in many others where you are not manufacturing a product but rather providing a service, the fully burdened cost of human capital is the biggest expense your company has. What I also realized was that for all the things we look at through the lens of ROI, the dollars of investment we made in our people was not one of them. When we think about people, performance, and the value we do or do not get in return on a per-person basis, we tend to get pulled into "the storytelling trap," a trap of excuses and reasons for underperformance that leads to tolerating mediocrity and underperformance for far too long.

When I started looking at people, the fully burdened investment I was making in each of them, and the Profit per X model, I started to realize that I needed to get very clear, for each unique role in my company, on what outcome they produced that was the single most critical outcome, within their control, that would prove to me I was getting a reasonable ROI for a given individual to be the right person in the role.

Once I could answer that question, I could begin to measure and track data and outcomes that I could share with employees and use to help them clearly understand whether or not they were winning in their role. This clarity helped us understand who was underperforming so that we could work with them through coaching, development, and support to get them to a level of meeting expectations for their Most Critical Outcome, producing positive and measurable ROI.

As we saw the success of this and the positive feedback from team members who finally got clarity on how they were actually performing in their roles, we decided to add MCOs to our version of the EOS Accountability Chart, another concept we learned from reading and following *Traction*. Adding this to the Accountability Chart was another evolution from EOS, but something that we found hugely valuable in further clarifying for team members what they were accountable for.

The hybrid version of EOS that I had self-implemented in North American Veneer served us well. As a result of the impact it had on that business, a startup in 2010, we grew to over seven million in annual revenue in just five years, and we did it with a small but aligned team of eighteen outstanding people. In 2015, we made the Inc. 5000 list of America's fastest-growing companies. I owe much of that success to the clarity I gained the first time I read *Traction* and to our customized self-implementation of EOS.

Wickman's evolution in creating EOS was an important improvement because it provided a simple, prescriptive, and linear approach that made it easier to implement and also more comprehensive than *Mastering the Rockefeller Habits*. At the same time, while evolved, it was also somewhat limiting in that it had a defined starting point, a singular path through the system, and an ending point (graduation), from which point forward you were on your own, without additional and evolving resources to support you as you grow. That is why I took the hybrid approach in my own business, working to break through some of those limitations.

In addition, EOS offered a finite toolbox of just twenty tools, which have not evolved since 2007. Deviating from the process or changing the tools has always been frowned upon, especially if you are working with an EOS Implementer. If the system or process of implementation does not fit an organization, the organization is generally expected to bend and morph to fit the system, not the other way around.

Scaling Up—Mastering the Rockefeller Habits 2.0

In 2014, on the heels of the significant success of EOS and *Traction*, Verne Harnish released *Scaling Up: Mastering the Rockefeller Habits 2.0*. Harnish's new book was a further evolution of business operating systems for two main reasons. It incorporated more tools and concepts around strategy and cash, which many people felt were weaknesses with EOS, and allowed the user to take a nonlinear approach instead of requiring the linear approach of EOS. This meant that users could choose the area where they felt the greatest struggles and work their way through the system in whichever order they believed was best for them. While still a basically prescriptive system, taking a nonlinear approach gave Scaling Up an advantage over EOS for those entrepreneurs who felt that EOS was a bit too restrictive and was boxing them in.

At this point, the world of business operating systems had gone from a handful of great tools and ideas with *Rockefeller Habits* to a more comprehensive, prescriptive, and linear system (EOS) to another comprehensive, prescriptive, but nonlinear system (Scaling Up.)

THE BIRTH OF A PRINCIPLED APPROACH

In 2015, on the heels of successfully self-implementing my own "customized" version of EOS, with the encouragement of my wife and trusted advisor, Elizabeth, I decided it was time to pursue a new future, and I began to slowly extract myself from North American Veneer. In May of 2015, I went through the training and became certified as an EOS Implementer. In the early days, because of my experience as a user and from my personal journey as an entrepreneur—one of great successes, devastating failures, and a "reincarnation" of sorts, which I wrote about in my 2017 best-selling book, *RISE: The Reincarnation of an Entrepreneur*—I was very successful within the EOS community. In both my second and third years, I broke the long-standing records for revenue generated as I ramped up early and fast. It was during that time that I met and grew to become very close friends with Greg Cleary and Duane Marshall, two other EOS Implementers who were among the most successful and tenured in the community.

Spending the years that I did as an EOS Implementer was incredibly helpful in my transition from a business owner to a business coach and ultimately to a Business Guide. During that time, I was able to learn a tremendous amount from Gino and other experienced members of the community, who provided thoughtful mentorship to me as I found my way forward on a completely different career path. I was able to learn new skills around meeting facilitation and how to manage a room. I even hired a facilitation coach who had a degree in psychology to help me further my growth and skill set to master my new role. I also earned certification through ForumSherpa, one of the leading organizations in the country training YPO and EO Forum Retreat Facilitators. My goal was never to facilitate forum retreats but rather to learn the skills of facilitation I had seen on so many of my own forum retreats when we would bring in trained outside facilitators. It was a critical stage in my personal growth and development, and I will be forever grateful to Gino and the EOS community for that stage of my journey.

During my time as an EOS Implementer, we all operated under a license agreement, which did not restrict implementers the flexibility to work outside the system. That meant we could technically teach our clients other tools and concepts as necessary to help them achieve their individual goals in ways that made the most sense, depending on their unique culture and industry. That flexibility was, in many ways, key to the collective success Greg, Duane, and I had relative to other EOS Implementers, although it was not looked favorably upon by leadership at EOS Worldwide.

Greg had even started the Millionaire Coaches Mastermind Group, which consisted of around twenty-five of the most successful and entrepreneurial EOS Implementers at that time. Under the freedom of the license agreement we had with EOS, we collaborated and shared ideas about how to make improvements and additions to the ways we were working with our clients. It allowed many of us to teach our clients additional concepts and provide them with new and improved tools so that we were able to evolve with them as they grew and add significant value for them beyond what otherwise should have been considered time for them to "graduate" from a traditional EOS Implementer.

As one example, I came up with an evolved concept of what EOS teaches as an accountability chart. One thing that had become clear to me throughout my career was that *the underlying cause of most frustrations between people is a result of unclear expectations.* While the EOS Accountability Chart helped to improve clarity over a traditional organizational chart, for many people, myself included, it was still a bit too vague. To solve that, I had been testing what I call MMOs® (Mission, Most Critical Outcome, and Obsessions®) for seats on an accountability chart. I'll go into deeper detail in the "Great People" chapter of this book, but when I began sharing and teaching our Mastermind Group about this evolved concept, many of them adopted it and began using it to help their clients establish clearer expectations and improve how employees could be coached and developed through a clear understanding of the Mission for their role, their Most Critical Outcome, and the handful of things they needed to constantly obsess about to be successful.

In May 2018, after scaling EOS from one to nearly two hundred EOS Implementers, Wickman sold a majority stake in the company to a private equity firm. It was the month of my third anniversary with EOS, and as is often the case with private equity in charge, things began to change. Late in 2019, EOS Worldwide began a transition to a franchise organization. While this was a smart and understandable move to make for the private equity group that purchased EOS in terms of improving their valuation over time, the franchise agreement removed many of the freedoms that we had, including the ability to be flexible with our clients to meet their needs. It also forced franchisees to be purely focused on nothing beyond the existing twenty EOS tools. From our perspective, this would significantly devalue our work with our clients, and if Greg, Duane, and I were going to continue putting our clients first, then we could not move forward as franchisees. Our values were no longer aligned with the organization where we had achieved so much success and helped so many.

NEXT LEVEL GROWTH AND PINNACLE BUSINESS GUIDES ARE BORN

"Never be so sure of what you have that you wouldn't take something better."

—CHRIS VOSS[7]

In November of 2019, after Greg and Duane had parted ways with EOS, and at a time when I was seriously questioning if I would continue under the coming franchise system, the three of us met for a long weekend at my home in Phoenix to share thoughts and ideas about what was going to be next for us all.

We spent the weekend working off of portable whiteboards by our pool and ideated on how we could take everything we had learned over our careers, break the mold of the typical, prescriptive systems, and create a flexible framework based on principles that would solve the common frustration with business operating systems being too "rigid." It was that weekend that the concept of a principled approach was born, as we aligned around five specific principles which, if an organization would remain focused on and relentlessly work to improve, would lead to great outcomes while providing significant flexibility within a framework.

---

7 Author discussed with Chris Voss at Genius Network Annual Event, Phoenix, AZ, November 9, 2024.

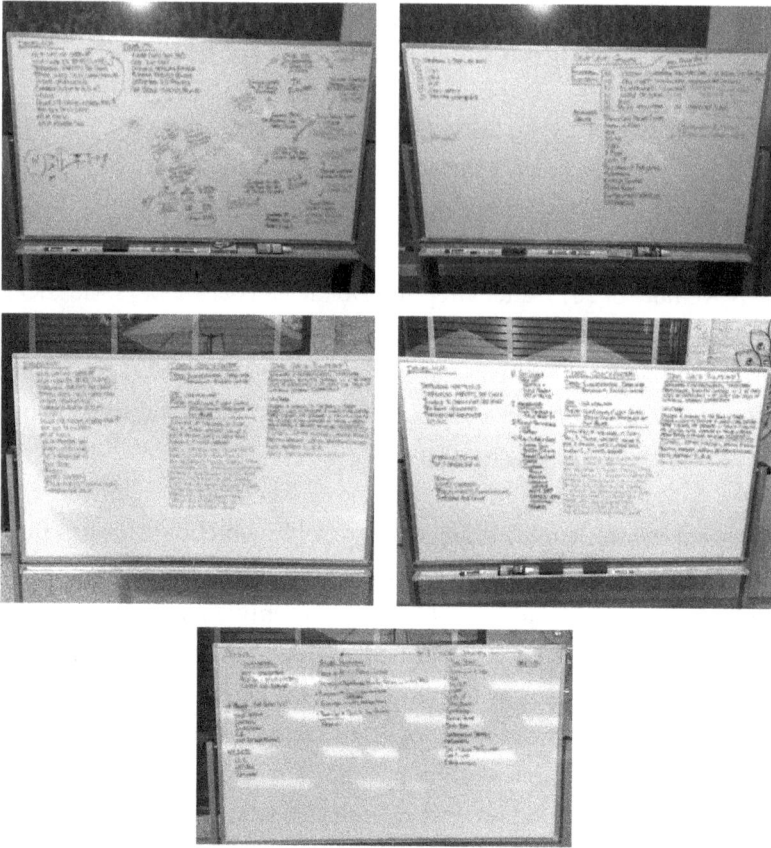

Figure 2.3
Images of the original whiteboards where Duane, Greg, and
Michael began to design a new, principled approach

In the beginning, Greg, Duane, and I set out to form a partnership, and my official role was going to specifically focus on leading from the finance seat, while Duane would focus on operations and Greg on marketing, business development, and recruiting. The three of us worked together to build and create the initial framework and the early-stage foundational tools, many of which were rooted in our collaboration with the Millionaire Coaches Mastermind Group.

Due to a personal family tragedy earlier that year, I had to temporarily disengage from my formal role before the formation of the legal entity that became Pinnacle Business Guides. As it worked out, I was not able to make my return until the legal entity had already been formed, and my rejoining as a third partner was no longer feasible. To keep things simple and collaborative between us, we agreed that I would continue to build my own brand, Next Level Growth, and at the same time continue as an active member of the Pinnacle community, continuing to help in the co-creation of tools to help our clients thrive. This collaboration both protected our friendships and prevented what would have been a nightmarish process of trying to unpack what co-created intellectual property (IP) belonged to whom and how IP would be treated going forward.

In 2020, Pinnacle Business Guides and Next Level Growth entered the market as the newest evolutions in the world of business operating systems. Both are principle-based and flexible, not prescriptive, making them more about the user and the outcomes desired than about the system itself. With Pinnacle and Next Level Growth, as with EOS and Scaling Up, the user gets a business operating system based on a core set of fundamentals. However, with Pinnacle and Next Level Growth, the resulting system is custom-tailored to fit, as opposed to a more rigid and prescriptive system requiring the user to adjust to fit the system.

Since that time, Next Level Growth has expanded to an elite team of Partners and Business Guides working with clients across the country.

FROM PRESCRIPTIVE TO PRINCIPLED— WHY IT MATTERS

Notice that I refer to Next Level Growth as a "principled approach." This is something that my friend, Mark Whitmore, wrote about in a post on LinkedIn: "I'm thinking about the differences between prescriptive and principled—how the one is a list of actions, and the other is a set of ideas on which to build something. The first, prescription, tells you what to do regardless of who you are. Generic. Paint by number. Plug and play. There is no room for dynamism—simply pull these levers and follow these instructions, and you will get these results. Check-the-box predictability."[8]

A principled approach, however, opens up a wide array of possibilities. While a principled approach still requires basic fundamentals, it allows the user to be creative and select the right tools and concepts to achieve the principle based on what is right for the organization, regardless of the source of those tools or concepts.

> *A principled approach is entrepreneurial. It also presumes that the entrepreneur ultimately knows what is best for his or her organization, versus a prescriptive system, which presumes that the system and its creator know what is best for **every** organization.*

For many smaller organizations, a prescriptive system is good enough. But if you have never been challenged and mentored to think with a 10X mindset, if you're not sure what really is possible for you and your business, *if you want to build something truly elite*, you will eventually need the freedom, flexibility, and creativity that comes with a principled approach and an Expert Guide (think of a Guide like a sherpa, helping you up Mount Everest). That is something you rarely find with a prescriptive system.

---

8 Mark Whitmore, "I'm thinking about the differences between prescriptive and principled…," LinkedIn post, May 2024, https://www.linkedin.com/posts/mark-whitmore-lodestone_sunday-morning-in-northern-ireland-im-sitting-activity-7185232637127540736-I_oW?utm_source=share&utm_medium=member_desktop.

In fact, one of a number of key differentiators comes from our one-phrase strategy, "*Experience Matters.*" When I use the term "Expert Guide" above, it is intentional. Many coaching organizations have a very low bar for becoming a coach. It is common that if you're willing to write the check to join, you're in. At Next Level Growth, all of our Guides have, at a minimum, been the owner, CEO, or president of an organization with at least ten million dollars in revenue and fifty or more employees. It's part of how we protect our brand and, even more importantly, how we ensure that the Guides who represent our brand have the significant real-world experience to be able to "sherpa" our client companies all the way to the summit of the business mountains they are climbing.

Pinnacle and Next Level Growth are founded on the same five basic principles that have been around for centuries and will be around for many more to come, with some minor modifications and variations in each of our tactical approaches, which has allowed us both to evolve from our original foundation and become increasingly unique in the tactical tools and concepts we provide. But in the end, it isn't about which tools and concepts you choose to implement. Instead, it is about you being focused on the right things to ultimately get the *big outcomes* you want. More than just helping you get a better Return on Investment from your business, it is ultimately about you earning a meaningful Return on Life.

At Next Level Growth, we call this framework *the Five Obsessions of Elite Organizations.*

FIVE OBSESSIONS OF
ELITE ORGANIZATIONS®

GREAT PEOPLE
•
INSPIRING PURPOSE
•
OPTIMIZED PLAYBOOKS
•
CULTURE OF PERFORMANCE
•
GROWING PROFITS & CASH FLOW

Figure 2.4

At our core, everything we do at Next Level Growth is about helping entrepreneurs and their leadership teams build elite organizations by learning, operationalizing, and executing a disciplined focus on *Great People*, aligned around and driven by an *Inspiring Purpose*, consistently training on, executing, and improving *Optimized Playbooks*, in a *Culture of Performance*, while proactively *Growing Profit and Cash Flow*. These are the Five Obsessions of Elite Organizations.

If you need a few examples of how dedication to the underlying and time-tested principles of the Five Obsessions of Elite Organizations can create astounding results, just consider some of the world's premier entrepreneurial leaders. No one can deny that Apple under Steve Jobs exploded in growth beyond anyone's expectations to become a global leader in communication, computer science, and so many other aspects of the technology we all depend on. Consider Elon Musk's pioneering of previously unimaginable innovations to change the way we not just drive, with Tesla, but also how we prepare for an uncertain future with SpaceX and Starlink. Think about Sir Richard Branson and how he scaled from a startup student magazine in 1966 to later launch Virgin Records and now lead the Virgin Group, a multinational conglomerate that oversees more than 400 companies. Research how, in 2006, Allan Mulally took over Ford Motor Company, which was facing bankruptcy and known for its toxic culture, and turned it around to create a thriving, healthy organization and the largest automobile company in the United States.

I've studied these entrepreneurs and many, many other groundbreaking leaders like them. One thing I discovered is that at their core, they all built their success by surrounding themselves with great people, guiding them through an inspiring purpose, systemizing and optimizing their processes, establishing a high-performing culture, and growing profits and cash flow that allowed them to reinvest, grow and accomplish extraordinary things... And the real wonder of this is that they all did so *in their own unique ways.* This is further evidence that the principles behind the framework of the Five Obsessions are valid and highly effective. All you need to do now is to figure out how to create the system that will accomplish your vision of success in your own organization.

This book will show you that path, and it is a path that begins with *Great People*, the first of the Five Obsessions of Elite Organizations.

Chapter 3

OBSESSION #1: GREAT PEOPLE

"Great vision without great people is irrelevant."

—JIM COLLINS

Lauren Bailey, co-founder and CEO of Upward Projects, the hospitality group behind the restaurant brands Postino, Windsor, Churn, Federal Pizza, and Joyride, was frustrated. It was the summer of 2017, and we were at The Henry, a popular meeting spot among entrepreneurs in Scottsdale, Arizona. The company that she had started with Craig DeMarco just eight years earlier had already grown to a total of twelve locations, with seven of those being its flagship concept, Postino.

In a nutshell, Upward Projects was in the final stages of securing a private equity deal, which they eventually closed in November of that year. The stakes were high, and growth was expected. Upward Projects would need to further accelerate its growth trajectory at a time when the organization was already beginning to grow at a faster pace than its leadership team could keep up with. This is a very common challenge that high-growth companies face. The first stage of growth is built with a team of people who are there from the start. They are the doers, the grinders. They are the ones who pulled the all-nighters to help the founder succeed in the early stages and get the company off the ground. In many cases, the growth of the company eventually reaches a point where the experience and skill sets that were needed in the early days are no longer sufficient for the future pace of growth and scale. This is where many organizations get stuck. We tend to see this happen most often somewhere between fifty to one hundred million in revenue, but it can happen at many different stages along a company's growth curve.

Lauren was at exactly this place with Upward Projects. Her leadership team had lots of experience and tenure with the company and had done an outstanding job of growing the organization to its current scale. Postino was clearly the growth engine, and Lauren knew that with the right people and the right focus, it had the potential to become a nationally recognized brand. At the same time, as with most entrepreneurs, there were so many doubts and so many questions.

As we started our work together in November of 2017, we began to clarify Lauren's vision for the organization. We started with what we call "The Summit." If you think of growing a business like climbing a mountain, you need to start by getting clear on what mountain you're climbing and what the summit of that mountain will look like. As the conversation goes between Alice and the Cheshire Cat in *Alice in Wonderland*, if you don't know where you're going, any road will take you there.

With her team's help, Lauren and the Upward Projects leadership team defined their Summit as: "*By the end of 2025, we will be a nationally recognized brand with 35 Postino locations.*" We added some qualitative language around what that would look like and what it would mean to be "*nationally recognized,*" and the vision of the Summit, while very far in the distance, began to provide some clarity and direction.

One thing that became clear to Lauren was that while some of the people around the table in those early meetings had done an outstanding job of helping her grow the business to those first seven Postino locations and were culturally great fits, it was going to take a different team of people, with different skills, to go from seven locations to thirty-five. She realized that growing the business five times its current size in just eight years would require people with vastly different experiences and perspectives.

Over the course of the next few years, Lauren remained very focused not only on her vision but also on making sure she found the right "who" for each key executive seat to help her through every stage of growth that was coming. This is an area where many entrepreneurs get trapped. They have so much love and loyalty for the people who helped them through the first phases of growth that they hang on too long when the needs of their business are growing at a faster pace than their people can grow, and as a result, the business stalls. It is what Jocko Willink and Leif Babin describe in their book, *The Dichotomy of Leadership*, as the "Ultimate Dichotomy."

> There are limitless dichotomies in leadership, and a leader must carefully balance these opposite forces. But none are as difficult as this: to care deeply for each individual member of the team while at the same time accepting the risks necessary to accomplish a mission... If leaders develop overly close relationships with their people, they may not be willing to [hold those people accountable] to do what is necessary to accomplish a [goal]. They may not have the wherewithal to [move on from] individuals with whom they have relationships, even if it is the right move for the good of the [organization].[9]

---

9 Jocko Willink and Leif Babin, *The Dichotomy of Leadership* (St. Martin's Press, 2018), 15.

The other thing that happens, and often ends badly, is that the very reason the entrepreneur hangs on to those people too long, the love and loyalty, begins to fade. As the organization stalls, the entrepreneur's frustration rises. The team members who are not keeping up with the growth of the business also grow frustrated as they feel the pressure of knowing they are not performing. As everyone's frustrations build, the pressure inside the team and the organization is also building, and eventually, the team chemistry will suffer, which will lead to further erosion of performance. That will accelerate the breakdown in team chemistry, and a downward spiral will begin to take over.

While it may seem counterintuitive, it can actually be kind to help a team member transition out of an organization when the organization's velocity is growing at a faster rate than their ability to keep up. At Next Level Growth, we strongly believe that everyone deserves an opportunity to be coached up and that every leader in an organization has to be focused on their role as a coach. However, when people cannot be coached up fast enough to keep up with the organization's needs, or when they simply lack the aptitude to level up as needed to meet new demands of their role, they need to be gracefully coached into another role or coached out. If someone was a great operations leader from one to ten locations but not able to level up to meet the demands of the organization at twenty to thirty locations, they would be much more successful and likely much happier either moving into a regional director role or going to work for another organization with one or two locations that is trying to get to ten.

In Lauren's case, her first new hire was to move from a controller on the executive team to a CFO. To level up her finance team, she brought in a CFO with experience at two different and larger hospitality companies who also had extensive experience with investor relations. Prior to that, she had a controller who was outstanding but did not yet have the level of experience and skills needed to be the CFO in the environment they were moving into. In this particular case, the controller transitioned off the leadership team, stayed with the organization, became a direct report to the new CFO, and has continued to grow and flourish as a key member of a powerful finance team. Since that time, she has worked her way up to senior corporate controller, and with everything she has learned under the mentorship of the CFO, I wouldn't be surprised to see her eventually becoming a CFO herself.

To bring in someone who had operational leadership experience at a larger scale and would be able to help the team become a nationally recognized brand, Lauren later brought in a rock star COO with over twenty years of executive operations experience at P. F. Chang's and Shake Shack. Again, by making a key investment in someone who has already been where she wanted to go, she was elevating the team exponentially.

When the vision for 2025 grew from thirty-five locations to fifty, Lauren knew she needed to upgrade her development team. Again, thinking big and being bold, she brought in a chief development officer who had previous experience with both Chipotle Mexican Grill and CAVA.

Of all the entrepreneurs I've worked with, Lauren is an extraordinary example of an entrepreneur who took big, bold steps to surround herself with the people she would need based on where she wanted to go rather than focusing on where she was. And it paid off. As of the publishing of this book, Postino has grown from seven locations when we first started working together to more than forty locations, and it is on its way to fifty in the next two years. They reached their original Summit of thirty-five locations ahead of schedule, and with locations currently in Arizona, California, Colorado, Georgia, North Carolina, Tennessee, and Texas, they are well on their way to becoming a national brand.

YOUR A-PLAYERS ARE FREE

Your A-Players are free, and they come with interest-free financing. This is something that my friend and co-author of the 2023 book *The Path to the Pinnacle,* Greg Cleary, and I have been saying for years.

Think about it. Every time you upgrade a position in your company from being filled by an underperformer to an A-Player, the marginal value of the A-Player far outweighs the marginal cost of the upgrade. At the same time, you likely pay your team members over twenty-four to twenty-six pay periods without interest, so while you are essentially financing the investment in the new A-Players, much of their value begins to come within the first few months of you bringing them on board. With that as context, let's dive into the first of the Five Obsessions of Elite Organizations, *Great People.*

WHAT IS AN A-PLAYER?

The definition of an A-Player will vary somewhat from one organization to another, but the way I like to define it follows a logic I learned twenty years ago when I studied *Topgrading* by Brad Smart. For the purposes of this book, I will be using the following definitions from *Topgrading*:

A-Player

- *Top 10 percent performers:* A-Players are the top 10 percent of talent available for a specific position, not just within your company but in the entire market.
- *High performers and high potentials:* These individuals consistently exceed expectations, demonstrate strong leadership, and contribute significantly to the organization's

goals. They are also aligned with the company's culture and values.

- *Growth-oriented:* A-Players are highly motivated, proactive, and adaptable. They constantly seek ways to improve themselves and their teams.
- *Retention-focused:* These employees typically stay with organizations that challenge and support them, offering opportunities for further development.

B-Player

- *Adequate performers:* B-Players are solid, reliable employees who meet expectations but rarely exceed them. They usually make up a large portion of the workforce.
- *Steady but not exceptional:* While B-Players are competent and contribute positively to the organization, they do not drive the high-impact results that A-Players do.
- *Limited growth potential:* These employees are typically less ambitious about career advancement or lack the skills to progress significantly. They perform well in stable roles but may struggle in rapidly changing environments.
- *Culturally aligned but less driven:* B-Players generally fit the company culture but are less likely to push themselves or others toward innovation or change.

C-Player

- *Underperformers:* C-Players are employees who consistently underperform or fail to meet expectations. They may have the wrong skills for the role or lack the motivation to succeed.
- *Misaligned with company culture:* Often, C-Players struggle to fit into the company's culture or fail to contribute positively to team dynamics.

- *Negative impact:* These individuals can hinder team performance and morale, dragging down the organization by requiring disproportionate management attention and resources.
- *Not a long-term fit:* The goal is to either develop or replace C-Players, as they pose a risk to achieving the company's long-term goals.

A-Potential

A-Potential refers to individuals who may not currently be A-Players in their roles but demonstrate the characteristics and potential to become A-Players in the future. You can identify employees with A-Potential by looking among your B's and occasionally your C's for the following five traits:

1. High Capacity for Growth

- *Learning agility:* A-Potential individuals are quick learners, able to pick up new skills and adapt to changing circumstances. They show the ability to thrive in more complex or demanding roles over time.
- *Track record of improvement:* They demonstrate a history of continuous development and have progressively taken on more responsibilities or shown the ability to step up in critical situations.

2. Cultural Alignment

- *Values match:* These individuals strongly align with the company's values, mission, and culture, which is essential for long-term success in the organization.
- *Leadership qualities:* Even if they are not currently in leadership positions, A-Potential candidates often display

leadership traits such as initiative, resilience, and emotional intelligence.

3. Drive and Motivation

- *Ambition and career aspirations:* A-Potential individuals are highly motivated to grow within the company and take on more significant roles. They seek out challenges and express a clear desire to achieve more.
- *Commitment to excellence:* They are driven to consistently improve their own performance, as well as the performance of their teams or departments, showing the work ethic and focus needed for A-Player status.

4. Adaptability

- *Change readiness:* A-Potential employees are flexible and adaptable to new opportunities or changes within the organization. They thrive in dynamic environments and can easily shift gears as needed.
- *Problem-solving mindset:* They show strong problem-solving capabilities and a proactive approach to tackling challenges, which indicates future success in more complex or strategic roles.

5. Future Leadership Material

- *Leadership development potential:* A-Potential individuals are seen as candidates for future leadership roles because of their ability to inspire others, take initiative, and make decisions that align with the company's long-term goals.
- *Capacity for strategic thinking:* While they may currently be involved in tactical or operational roles, these

individuals demonstrate the ability to think strategically and are preparing to move into roles that require broader organizational insight.

Topgrading, and all of us at Next Level Growth, emphasizes the importance of identifying your A-Potential team members because these individuals, when nurtured and given the right opportunities, can develop into the company's future A-Players, filling critical leadership positions as the organization grows.

AN A-PLAYER CULTURE

Rudyard Kipling begins his famous poem "The Law of the Jungle" as follows:

> "Now this is the Law of the Jungle—as old and as true as the sky;
>
> And the Wolf that shall keep it may prosper, but the Wolf that shall break it must die.
>
> As the creeper that girdles the tree trunk, the Law runneth forward and back—
>
> For the strength of the Pack is the Wolf, and the strength of the Wolf is the Pack."[10]

On your journey to building an elite organization, "…the strength of the Pack is the Wolf," means that you must commit to and remain disciplined about developing, recruiting, and retaining *Great People*. These are people who advocate for your values and culture, who have

---

10 Rudyard Kipling, "The Law of the Jungle," in *The Second Jungle Book*, 1894.

the skills and drive to consistently perform to a high standard, and who passionately embrace your cause as an organization. At the same time, "…and the strength of the Wolf is the Pack," means that you must prioritize the highest level team you are on as the most important team. Leaders cannot prioritize the teams they lead over the highest team in which they work, or they will end up lobbying for their constituents, like Congress, rather than for the good of the organization and its cause.

For example, at a leadership team level, where you might have your director of sales and director of operations both participating with this as their highest-level team, they must prioritize the leadership team over the needs of the departmental teams they lead. This is a concept Patrick Lencioni describes as *Team One*. There is a natural tendency for leaders to prioritize the teams they lead over the highest team on which they serve. They do this because they hired the people on their team, they work closely together, and they share the same skill sets and interests. While their intentions are usually good, it is actually very harmful to the organization because when those leaders come together to meet as a leadership team, they will naturally act like Congress and lobby for their constituents rather than the greater good of the organization. When they do this, they are not only working against what is best for the organization, but they also create silos within the organization as they set their team members up to feel more like they are battling with other departments than they are collaborating and working toward a common goal.

Note: To watch Patrick Lencioni describe Team One in greater detail, visit our YouTube channel at YouTube.com/@NextLevelGrowth and visit the "Client Favorites" playlist.

You must protect the health and cohesiveness of your team at all costs and above all else. That requires you to have an *A-Player System*.

THE A-PLAYER SYSTEM

Most organizations have several "potential" A-Players already inside the company. The problem is that they either have no consistent way to assess individual performance, or they have a system that is so complicated or requires so much time and energy from leaders and managers that it is simply not effective in driving an obsession around coaching, development, and filling the organization with *Great People*.

At Next Level Growth, we work with all of our clients to develop their own customized A-Player System. The A-Player System has a handful of key components, which include:

- Core Values
- Next Level Accountability Chart®
- Onboarding System (discussed in Chapter 5)
- Quarterly Calibrations (discussed in Chapter 6)
- Coaching Plans (discussed in Chapter 6)

CORE VALUES—THE FOUNDATION
OF YOUR CULTURE

Many organizations have core values, and some of them have great core values. The concept of core values has become very common and, in many cases, very cliché. In *Traction*, Gino Wickman does a great job of breaking down a simple process of discovery, rather than creation, to understand and begin to articulate your core values. This is a very similar process to the one we teach our clients at Next Level Growth.

Start with your leadership team and ask everyone to make a list of three people, ideally people already inside the organization but not on the leadership team, who, if you were going to restart the business from scratch, would be the top three people you would absolutely want to take with you to start over. Put all the names on a single list, ideally on a large whiteboard or a flip chart.

Next, looking at the list of names, ask everyone to make a second list of the most common characteristics, qualities, and traits of those people that are the reasons they are on the list. Once everyone has made their list, transfer all of their answers to the board. What you will start to see is that among the list of traits, just a handful of themes emerge. Once all of this is on the board, use different colored markers and go through the traits together, color-coding them based on the common themes.

Once you have the list of traits color-coded, rewrite them in groups based on color. Once we've done this, we like to draw a box around each grouping. From there, you can have a discussion about the word or phrase that captures the essence of what is in the box. Sometimes, it is one of the words or phrases from the exercise, and other times, seeing all the words and phrases together brings something even better to mind.

Here is an example of all the words and phrases grouped together from doing this exercise with one of our clients:

Can-Do Attitude	Selfless	Easy to Communicate with	Eager to Learn & Grow
Does What It Takes	Trustworthy	Never Complains	Seeks to Improve
Self-Starter	Honesty	Composed under Stress	Always Learning
Perseverance	Integrity	Helpful	Coachable
	Dependable	Good Attitude	Good Attitude
	Good Work Ethic	Caring	
		Team Player	

Figure 3.1

From those four boxes, the "discovered" core values this organization came up with were: *Driven, Dependable, Team Players,* and *Passion for Growth.* We asked our client to put them in a "voice" that felt inclusive and collaborative, and we also encouraged them to include verbs in each short statement as these are really about actions that they wanted to see in people's behaviors to be able to know that they would be the right fit for their culture. In this case, they ended with:

- We Are Driven
- We Are Dependable
- We Are Team Players
- We Are Passionate about Growth

In terms of how they now speak about and introduce their core values, they simply turned it into a sentence. *We are driven, dependable team players who are passionate about growth.* People in the organization see it being lived out from the top down, and they are embracing what it means to be part of such a great and aligned community on the relentless journey to the summit of their business mountain.

Once you have your core values, you will need to confirm the behaviors that will define what those values look like in your unique organization. With that clarity, the final step is to confirm that these are, in fact, the right values. Begin by asking yourselves, *If we use these core values in our hiring, firing, coaching, and rewarding, and can get everyone to align their behaviors with these values, will that be transformational and beneficial to the organization going forward?* If the answer is yes, then you have likely landed on the right genuine and authentic values.

The next and final step of the exercise is to have an open and honest discussion among the leadership team about how each leadership team member's behaviors and interactions are aligning, or not aligning, with these organizational core values. It is important to ensure that if you are going to agree to and promote these values within the organization, the leaders must set the standard of what it looks like to live these behaviors. As John Maxwell wrote about in *The 21 Irrefutable Laws of Leadership*, the "Law of the Lid" describes how a leader's limitations will set the limitations, or lid, not only on the leader but on the organization. Your team members will naturally not go beyond what they see in their leaders, so if one of your core values is dependable, you cannot expect that your employees will be more dependable than your least dependable leader.

At Next Level Growth, our core values are Take Ownership, Be Resourceful, Have a Thirst for Learning, and Be Fun to Work With. We talk about these values often, and we use the specific wording of our values both when acknowledging a positive behavior or challenging one that needs correction. Sometimes, when I'm asked how to do something that is clearly a part of our documented onboarding and training and that the team member should know how to find on their own without asking me, I'll respond by saying something like, "*If you were being resourceful, how could you find the answer to that question?*" It's a way to remind the person that, in the moment, they are not being resourceful. The more consistently I do this, the faster they understand where they are falling short in that value and the more likely they are to self-correct in the future.

On the other side of that same coin, when somebody does something that is a great example of embracing one of our values, I will reference the specific value when I acknowledge my appreciation. One of our newer Guides and I were recently talking through some facilitation techniques around a specific issue, and he referenced several things related to the topic that he had seen in our training videos. It was a great example of taking ownership of his own training, and it also showed me that he was being resourceful, so I mentioned those specific values and thanked him for being so engaged and resourceful in how he was taking ownership of his onboarding.

FROM AN ORG CHART TO AN ACCOUNTABILITY CHART

Also in *Traction*, Wickman made a significant improvement to the well-known org chart (organizational chart) when he introduced the idea of an Accountability Chart. The purpose was to clarify the roles and responsibilities for every seat in the company by adding a few short words or phrases as bullet points in the box for each seat.

In the example of a Sales & Marketing Leadership seat from the book *Traction*, those bullet points are LMA, Sales Goal, Selling, Marketing, and Sales & Marketing Process. While a good step in the right direction, when I implemented EOS in my own business, I felt this was an oversimplification and needed to be stronger if it was truly going to set clear expectations to help leaders and managers effectively identify the right people for the right seats, and either coach people up, or coach people out when they were not performing to expectations.

All of the companies I have worked with over the years have heard me say that *I believe the underlying cause of most of our frustrations is based on unclear expectations.* This applies in all areas of life, and especially in the relationships between a leader and their direct reports.

The Next Level Accountability Chart

This led to the creation and evolution of what we teach at Next Level Growth as the *Next Level Accountability Chart.* The critical difference, and in fact, the key value of the Next Level Accountability Chart is in establishing what we call MMOs, an acronym that stands for Mission, Most Critical Outcome, and Obsessions®. With MMOs in place for every seat, both the leader and their direct report will have absolute clarity on what is expected of them so that they can truly understand if they are in the right seat and, if necessary, get the coaching and development they need and be clear about where they need it.

Let me share an example using the same Sales & Marketing Leadership position mentioned from *Traction* above. First, to the Mission.

Establishing a Clear Mission

We define the "Mission" for a seat as a one-sentence description of the consistent, high-level deliverable a person in a seat on the Next Level Accountability Chart must achieve to be successful. Think about a typical executive team with a chief executive officer, a marketing and sales leader, an operations leader, and a finance leader. The Mission of each position should support the Mission of the person to whom they report.

For example, the CEO who reports to either the owners or the Board of Directors (or is themselves the owner) might have a mission to "Grow the Enterprise Value by guiding and ensuring the execution of the long-term strategy while maintaining an on-brand culture." This mission encompasses many things, but over time, we can evaluate how well our long-term strategy is both being executed and how well it is working. We can measure our Enterprise Value, and we can tell if our culture is or is not on-brand. That creates a clearer path to outcomes-based accountability.

From there, let's look at a possible Mission for our marketing and sales leader. For this role, you might decide on a mission to "*Consistently grow target market lead generation and conversion to meet or exceed revenue goals.*" It is a simple statement and should be fairly obvious, but this is also high-level and highly measurable, which creates clarity and accountability. We have a budget for the year based on achieving a specific revenue goal, and if this leader drives sufficient target market growth in lead generation and successfully converts the leads at the conversion rate necessary to meet our budget, the company will likely meet or exceed its revenue goals. As a result, we can measure, track, and discuss performance around this mission on a consistent basis.

Moving on to the operations leader, if we assume this company is in the home services industry, the Mission might be something like, "*Ensure the on-brand and on-budget execution of all projects, in a timely manner, while maintaining a safe and healthy working environment.*" Again, this encompasses a lot, but it is an overarching statement that has multiple components that can be objectively evaluated.

Lastly, looking at the finance leader, one of the most common Missions we see with our clients for this role is "*Timely and accurate delivery of financial reporting, analysis, budgeting and forecasting.*" If the finance leader consistently delivers on that mission, the rest of the team will have all the information they need, when they need it, to make educated and informed decisions that help them lead the organization toward its Summit.

When you step back and look at each of these Missions, if the marketing and sales leader, the operations leader, and the finance leader all consistently execute their Missions, then the CEO's Mission of growing the Enterprise Value by guiding and ensuring the execution of the long-term strategy while maintaining an on-brand culture is much more likely to be successfully achieved.

Most Critical Outcome®

The second component of the Next Level Accountability Chart, the Most Critical Outcome (MCO), is defined as the single most important and measurable outcome for a function. At the leadership team level, the MCO is almost always a lagging indicator and typically should be tracked on a monthly team scorecard, by person. The two to four primary drivers of each MCO are usually measurable leading activities and should be tracked on your team's weekly scorecard. The Most Critical Outcome should both prove success in achieving the mission and also answer the following question: "*If you were asked to measure one thing that most accurately proves you are getting a return on investment for the fully burdened human capital cost of a specific person in a given seat, what would you measure?*"

In the case of our executive team, as shown in the example above, most CEOs have an MCO of Enterprise Value Dollars to Goal. In some cases, I have seen Return on Invested Capital to Goal as a CEO's MCO, but in any case, if the Mission is about growing the value of the business, the MCO has to be the outcome that you measure to prove growth in value relative to a specific goal.

With the CEO's MCO established, the marketing and sales leader will likely have an MCO as obvious as Revenue Dollars to Goal (budget or forecast, depending on which one you use). If the company is consistently meeting or exceeding revenue goals and forecasts, it is very likely that the marketing and sales leader is performing at a high level in leading their team and generating a sufficient Return on Investment for the compensation they are being paid.

For the operations leader, depending on how your financials are constructed and what specific things they have decision-making authority over, a typical MCO would be something like Gross Profit Percentage to Goal, Net Operating Income Percentage to Goal, or Net Income Percentage to Goal. Ultimately, it is the marketing and sales leader's job to go get the revenue dollars you need, and it is the operations leader's job to run a tight and efficient operation that meets the profitability goals as a percentage of revenue generated.

One thing I want to point out here is something that has evolved in our own thinking over time. Notice that the marketing and sales leader's MCO is measured in actual dollars, and the operations leader's is a percentage. In the early developmental stages of Most Critical Outcomes, we were coaching teams to set the operations leader's MCO in terms of real dollars as well, but we noticed a behavior that would often come from that which went against what Missions and Most Critical Outcomes are intended to do: drive the right focus and behaviors.

When we had situations where the revenue had fallen off track and behind budget, it soon became obvious to the team that the profit number, in terms of dollars, could not realistically be met, so the teams' focus on profit and being good stewards of financial resources would become diluted. If, instead, the operations leader was focused on meeting the goal as a percentage, then even if the company's revenue missed by 10 percent, if the operations lead acted quickly and decisively, they could often maintain or come very close to maintaining the percentage of profit budgeted. By having them focus more on the ratio of expenses to revenue, they could play their position with a different and more helpful mindset.

Lastly is the finance leader, which becomes a little more nuanced. The finance leader rarely has the authority to pull a lot of levers that impact revenue and profit, as their role is more rooted in analysis, reporting, and interpretation of data. I'm a big believer that at an executive level, your finance leader should have an MCO of Net Cash Flow Dollars to Goal. Here's my logic behind creating an MCO that they don't actually control:

Similar to setting an intention, the MCO should really help focus each team member in the organization. We want our finance leader to always be ahead of the company from a cash flow forecasting and analysis position. In the budgeting process, we want them to take the extra steps of not just a Profit and Loss budget, but also to dig into the "how" behind the Profit and Loss budget. We want them to be thinking about the balance sheet and Cash Flow impact. Every annual budget should be able to reasonably estimate cash flow to the point that we can establish some goals and parameters. With those goals established, by arming your finance leader with an MCO of Net Cash Flow Dollars to Goal, you are focusing them on cash flow forecasting, protecting the organization as it grows.

Every time I go through this exercise with my clients, I look at the finance leader and tell them that my intention with asking them to accept this MCO is that whenever they see a warning sign on the horizon, they are sounding alarms and getting everyone's attention so that decisions can be made long before cash gets tight and decisions have to be forced upon the organization.

In reality, if the marketing and sales leader meets their goal for revenue dollars, the operations leader meets their goal for Income Percentage, and the finance leader ensures we meet our goal for cash flow, the CEO will almost certainly meet their goal for Enterprise Growth Value.

This same logic holds true throughout the entire organization. If you build a single MCO into every position in the company, and every position's MCO is supportive of the MCO in the seat to which it reports, you will build a *fabulous economic engine* in your organization and become much more financially resilient and successful.

Defining Obsessions

Lastly, we come to Obsessions. Obsessions are defined as anywhere from two to six things that a seat-holder must obsess about on a daily basis to be successful (usually around four to six at a senior leadership level and as few as two to three for a front-line employee). While the EOS Accountability Chart uses just a single word or short phrase for each of the roles or responsibilities, we believe there is still too much ambiguity and room for interpretation and confusion. If you look at the example from *Traction* earlier in this section, it can be difficult to truly hold people accountable for "selling." What exactly does that mean in terms of how you measure a person's success?

When you have a clearly established Mission with the right MCO, the Obsessions become a strong way to align expectations around where a team member must focus to be successful at the level of an A-Player. For example, the Obsessions I often suggest as a starting point for a marketing and sales leader are:

1. Lead, Manage, Retain, and Hold My Team Accountable

I personally prefer to start with this Obsession for anyone in the organization who has a direct report. With this approach, we can specifically evaluate a team leader on how well they are *"leading"* the team. Is there dissension or harmony? There are things we can observe and use to provide feedback to help the leader improve if needed. We can look at how they *"manage"* the team on a daily basis and provide coaching and feedback. We can look at *"retention"* on the team. *Most people go to work for an organization but quit because of their boss.* If a team leader has trouble retaining their high performers, then they need to be coached in that area.

Some people would argue, and some systems suggest, that accountability is a by-product of leading and managing. While I agree in theory, in the real world, I have found that when leaders are not willing to have the tough conversations necessary to hold their teams accountable when needed, the teams underperform. Measuring how well a team leader holds their team accountable is actually not very difficult at all.

2. Own the Marketing and Sales Strategies, Plans, and Outcomes

If the person in this seat focuses their energy on getting the marketing and sales strategies right, developing and updating the right plans to execute on the strategy, and tracking outcomes to adjust where needed, we have them laser-focused on a strategic approach to growing our pipeline, conversion, and revenue. If, over time, they cannot get the right strategy and plan in place to achieve the desired outcome, they are likely not the right person for the seat.

With this obsession in place, when we work with teams who are not meeting their revenue goals, it allows us to ask the leadership team to share their marketing and sales strategy documents and their written sales plans for each individual sales team member with us so we can evaluate them and try to help. What often happens is that we get a response like, "*Well, we don't actually have them all documented.*" In that case, it is difficult to confirm that the members of the sales team really have clear expectations of what their sales plans are and how they are supposed to execute a well-defined strategy to grow revenues and meet growth goals.

3. Own the Marketing and Sales Process Playbooks and Execution

With the right strategies and plans in place, to be successful in this role, an A-Player will obsess about the playbooks and about making sure that everyone on the sales team is following them. So many times, when we start digging into a company's "sales playbook," we find that they really don't have one, and everyone on the sales team is more or less doing their own thing. With a strong leader in place, the team can develop some best practices and optimize how they run their sales plays to help improve conversion throughout the sales funnel and accelerate growth.

Think about your own organization. When you get a new lead or a new referral, if you watch how every one of them is handled, is it consistent? Does it happen every time the way that it needs to in order to create the highest likelihood of a positive outcome? Are there key points that your sales team needs to make in the very first communication? Do they consistently hit on those points? Do you have a consistent and well-trained way for team members to handle and overcome objections?

Remember the Paul Batalden quote from earlier: "Every system is perfectly designed to get the results it gets." If you are getting inconsistent results from your sales team, you have a system in place that is perfectly designed to create inconsistent results. You need a marketing and sales leader capable of creating, training, and enforcing a better system if you want better results.

4. Consistently Meet or Exceed Goals and Metrics

While this one may be implied, we like to include it anyway. If we're going to give our marketing and sales leader four things to obsess about on a daily basis, we want one of those to be their goals and metrics.

So, if on a daily basis, the director of marketing and sales truly obsesses about leading, managing, retaining, and holding their team accountable; owning the marketing and sales strategies, plans, and outcomes; owning their playbooks and execution; and meeting or exceeding their goals and metrics, they are very likely to be highly successful in the role, or else it will become very obvious, very fast, that they are not right for the seat.

When you establish a clear Mission, Most Critical Outcome, and Obsessions for every role in your organization, communicate those clearly, and coach people in each of those areas, you create de facto agreements. Like Harvey Mackay says, "Agreements prevent disagreements."[11] If you agree with me that *the underlying cause of most frustrations we have with people is a result of unclear expectations*, then use the Next Level Accountability Chart to create simple but clear expectations and reduce frustration throughout the organization.

---

11 Harvey Mackay, "70 Years of Brutally Honest Business Advice in 25 Mins | Harvey Mackay," Joe Polish, June 1, 2024, YouTube video, 25:08, https://youtu.be/Dppm6mH-DhM?si=OQQ_YsFGfhZA4vJl.

NEXT LEVEL ACCOUNTABILITY CHART— GOING DEEPER

Now that we have clarified what the marketing and sales leader is accountable for, let's look at how the seat for a direct report, perhaps an outside salesperson, might be established.

You may notice that each Obsession in the Next Level Accountability Chart contains a verb. That is because these obsessions are about taking action, and it is important to get the verbs right if you're going to create clarity. When we suggest the verb "own" for a leadership team member, what we mean by that is if something isn't working, and they own it, it is their job to fix it. If they get stuck, of course, the rest of the team is there to help, but the vast majority of the time, they should have the aptitude to fix what they own when it isn't getting the desired result, or they may be in the wrong seat.

For an outside sales seat, in light of the leader's mission, you might establish their supportive Mission as something like, "*Consistently grow and convert my pipeline to meet or exceed my individual goal for new revenue.*" This mission, when achieved, supports the mission of the person to whom they report. The corresponding MCO would likely then be "*New revenue dollars to individual goal.*"

When rolling out their Obsessions, you should start by looking at the seat to which they report. This holds true everywhere in your Next Level Accountability Chart. Since this person will have no direct reports, the Obsession around leading, managing, retaining, and holding their team accountable does not apply. They might, however, have an Obsession that stems from the second Obsession of their leader, and that might be to "*Follow and successfully execute my sales plan.*"

Notice that the verb changed to "follow." This is important because, for this person, you don't want them making up or modifying their sales plan without working with their leader. You want them to buy into the plan and then obsess about following and successfully executing it.

Another obsession might be *"Follow the Sales Process Playbook."* If the leader "owns" the Sales Process Playbook, you likely want the salespeople to obsess about "following" the Playbook.

Finally, as before, we like to suggest including the Obsession to *"Meet or exceed my goals and metrics."* It's really that simple and, at the same time, that powerful. Think about it. In your own organization, how consistently is the sales team doing a great job of those three things? In most organizations, it is very hit-and-miss.

When you have a salesperson in the field, if they will just obsess about executing on their individual sales plan, following the sales playbooks, and meeting or exceeding their goals and metrics, and if their boss has taken ownership of creating effective plans and playbooks, they have a much greater chance of being successful in their role. With this level of clarity, consistency, and focus, the employee wins, their leader wins, the company wins, and the customer wins. It is not the intensity of your efforts but the consistency of your efforts that leads to success.

For more help building your own A-Player System, be sure to consult with my clone at **AskMichaelErath.com**.

RIGHT PEOPLE, RIGHT SEATS—
GOOD TO GREAT, BUT NOT ELITE

Now that you have the foundational clarity and tools to begin filling your organization with *Great People* who share your values and have the skills and desire to perform their roles to a high standard, you need to capture their hearts. Over the course of my career, I've come to realize that if you are really obsessed about *Great People* in your organization, the "right people in the right seats" analogy made popular in *Good to Great* is missing one important thing. In order for people to truly be their best, they must also feel an emotional connection to an *Inspiring Purpose* behind what they do and what the organization stands for.

The analogy Collins uses is to think of your organization as a bus. You first have to get the right people, those who share your values, on the bus and the wrong people off the bus. Then you have to get those right people in the right seats, meaning in seats that are a good fit for them to perform to a high standard based on their skills and abilities. At Next Level Growth, we believe there is a third component required to go from good, to great, to elite.

Yes, we need our team members to share our behavioral core values. And yes, we need them to have the skill sets, experience, and desire to perform their roles at a high level. But when you add in the third element, that they form an emotional connection to their company's *Inspiring Purpose*, that is when they will bring the greatest effort, drive, passion, and creativity to their role. That is when they will resist silos in the organization and collaborate best with others because they no longer see what they do as a job, but rather as their contribution to a greater cause that inspires them.

When you have the right people in the right seats, and you inspire them in a way that allows an internal and purposeful connection to the organization to be formed, they will always bring more energy, passion, and creativity to their work because their connection to their work is not just rational, it is emotional. This is a key part of what we call an *Inspiring Purpose*, the second of the Five Obsessions of Elite Organizations.

Chapter 4

OBSESSION #2: AN INSPIRING PURPOSE

> "Those who truly lead are able to create a following of
> people who act not because they were swayed,
> but because they were inspired."
>
> —SIMON SINEK

Steve Jobs once said that the most powerful person in the world is the storyteller. Great stories capture our hearts and bring inspiration. When people are emotionally engaged and inspired, they will bring more discipline and passion to what they are doing. The power of the second obsession of elite organizations, an *Inspiring Purpose*, while often overlooked, is very real.

In his 2009 best-selling book, *Start with Why*, Simon Sinek states that people don't buy "what" you do; they buy "why" you do it. While I believe that statement is true in varying degrees depending on the product, I do believe it is a true statement, and I've seen clients with very commoditized products differentiate themselves through a clear and powerful "why." It is up to the leaders of an organization to discover their why and then ensure they can articulate it in a clear and inspiring way so that it not only drives external marketing and public relations (PR) but also fuels internal passion and engagement.

In total, there are twelve areas that we work on with our clients to build a clear framework around a robust marketing strategy that helps them communicate their *Inspiring Purpose*. Going deep into each of them would be a book of its own, and there are already plenty of great marketing books out there. For the purpose of this book, I'm going to focus on the specific components that you can clarify and use to help build internal team member engagement and alignment. When you have *Great People* in your organization, and you can capture their hearts and emotions with an *Inspiring Purpose*, that emotional connection to the organization will almost always lead to them bringing more passion, creativity, collaboration, and enthusiasm to the work that they do.

EMPLOYEE ENGAGEMENT AND AN INSPIRING PURPOSE

Think about it. What was your organization's marketing budget last year? What percentage of it was invested in marketing internally to your team members? What does that tell you about the value you place on inspiring and engaging your employees? What should you be investing to capture the hearts and passions of your teams?

At Next Level Growth, we use a combination of concepts from different thought leaders to help our clients articulate six key pillars of the internal aspect of their *Inspiring Purpose*. The first three, which I will focus on in this chapter, are a Just Cause, a Daily Purpose, and a Strategic Niche. When we incorporate this into Jim Collins's "hedgehog concept" by including an understanding of the organization's Profit per X (what drives their economic engine and will be discussed in Chapter 7) and then also overlay the business model as a flywheel, all of the components fall into place to help every employee in an organization understand how their specific role within the Next Level Accountability Chart is part of a bigger picture that advances the organization's Just Cause.[12] It also provides a strong framework for making better decisions.

From this, many of our clients will also go on to create what Collins refers to in his book *Great by Choice* as a SMaC Recipe. *SMaC* stands for Specific, Methodical, and Consistent and is defined as "a set of durable operating practices that creates a replicable, consistent success formula."[13] At Next Level Growth, our SMaC Recipe is something we call our *10 Promises* and clarifies how we operationalize our strategic differentiating concepts in ways that are durable and replicable. I'll share more on that near the end of this chapter.

> Note: To learn more in-depth about flywheels and SMaC Recipe, see *Good to Great*, Chapter 5, and *Great by Choice*, also by Jim Collins, Chapter 7.

DAILY PURPOSE—START WITH WHY

The second pillar of an *Inspiring Purpose*, which I will speak to first, is what we call an organization's Daily Purpose. It speaks to an organization's "why"—its origin story. When working with clients, we start here because we find that the order in which we go through a discovery

---

12 Jim Collins, "The Hedgehog Concept," jimcollins.com, accessed December 5, 2024, https://www.jimcollins.com/concepts/the-hedgehog-concept.html.

13 Jim Collins and Morten T. Hansen, *Great by Choice: Uncertainty, Chaos, and Luck—Why Some Thrive Despite Them All* (Harper Business, 2011).

process matters in terms of both accuracy and efficiency. We start with Daily Purpose, then use the clarity of that Daily Purpose, or "why," to uncover the Just Cause.

To begin to understand an organization's Daily Purpose, we like to ask the founder why they started the company. The answer must be framed in terms of what you do with the company for the people you serve, who can be external or internal, not that you started it to make money. It should be about outcomes that you produce and that you focus on achieving every day. Again, some founders realize that it is more about the people inside their business than their external customers or clients, and there is nothing wrong with that. Both can be, and in fact are, very important...but for the sake of your truest purpose, you must decide which is primary. This often takes several rounds of questioning the answers we receive and asking "why" over and over again until we get there.

Then, we turn to the team and ask them to articulate why, beyond money, they choose to stay at the company. What is it about the work they do, what outcomes they accomplish, that brings them joy and keeps them committed to the organization? As we work to get alignment among the answers, there is almost always an "aha" moment where the words become very clear.

DAILY PURPOSE—AN EXAMPLE

As an example, our "Why" at Next Level Growth is:

Helping Entrepreneurial Leaders Build Elite Organizations®

On our YouTube channel, there is a video of Nick Saban talking about five choices we have in life:

- You can be bad at what you do.
- You can be average at what you do.
- You can be good at what you do, which Saban says is probably God's expectation based on whatever talent He gave us.
- You can choose to be excellent.
- You can choose to be elite.

He goes on to say, "If you're going to be excellent or elite, you have to have a special discipline, focus, drive, and passion to do things at a high level and to a high standard all of the time, and without that, you're probably never going to be more than just good."[14]

When I first heard this, it resonated. When I looked back over my career, I saw that I had built good businesses. At times, for a little while, we were even excellent, but I never put all the pieces in place to build something truly elite. As I started thinking about companies I've worked with since becoming a Business Guide, using this lens of an elite organization helped frame how I looked at the best of the best companies and what they did differently that held the keys to their success. It was this short Nick Saban video that provided the spark that is at the core of our approach to the Five Obsessions of Elite Organizations.

Applying these five choices to things I had experienced was really the first time that the difference between a prescriptive system and a principled approach started to become clear to me. During my years as an EOS Implementer, I helped many organizations become good just based on their use of the foundational tools of the system. But for the ones who focused on the system and put primacy on purity to the system, most of them never got past good.

---

14 Nick Saban, "Nick Saban and the Mindset of Great People," Next Level Growth, September 2, 2023, YouTube video, 1:55, https://youtu.be/9MCVAFA9AM0?si=df7s80jzuA5leHOg.

OBSESSION #2: AN INSPIRING PURPOSE · 77

It was the companies where I could work in the margins and go beyond the basics of EOS, bringing in other tools and concepts from other systems and thought leaders, as well as things I had created on my own journey, which were the organizations that began to move more consistently from good to excellent or elite. In fact, this idea of going beyond and breaking out of the box is the story behind the Next Level Growth logo, which I will explain next, and an image of which you can find at NextLevelGrowth.com.

As I wrote about in Chapter 2, when I decided to part ways with EOS, they were going through their transition to a franchise model, and as part of that, were growing more and more focused on purity to the twenty tools of the EOS toolbox and making claims that the only thing clients needed were in the twenty tools. While I think the tools and the system are very good, I could not accept the mindset that one system has all the answers and purity to that system was the only way. It felt like a scarcity mindset and not very entrepreneurial. Leaving EOS, for me, was like breaking out of a box. Considering that EOS uses orange as its primary logo color, I wanted our logo to create a sense of breaking out of the orange box.

According to an article posted on Super Color Digital's website on the meaning of different colors, "The color blue represents both the sky and the sea and is associated with open spaces, freedom, intuition, imagination, inspiration, and sensitivity. Blue also represents meanings of depth, trust, loyalty, sincerity, wisdom, confidence, stability, faith, and intelligence."[15] The association between the color blue and the principled approach that I believed in come together in words from this description like freedom, imagination, inspiration, wisdom, and intelligence. These are all words that I associate with entrepreneurship

---

15 Super Color Digital, "The Psychology of Color," *Super Color Digital* (blog), July 1, 2019, https://www.supercolor.com/blog/psychology-of-color/.

and which I felt were being restricted by the purity pressure I had been living under.

With that, I set out to design a logo for my rebranding as Next Level Growth and chose blue as the primary color. I wanted to contrast that with the color orange and wanted the logo to show that, in fairness, there is growth to be had within the constraints of a prescriptive system, as represented by the orange bars growing from left to right inside the orange box. I also wanted to make the statement that to really create exponential growth and build something elite, you have to break out of the box, which is why the final bar in our logo is back to our primary color, blue, designed as a bar that is also an upward-pointing arrow, and which has broken through the box and is reaching toward the next level.

Our logo is a subtle representation of the "*why*" behind Next Level Growth—*Helping entrepreneurial leaders build elite organizations*—and is intended to be one more small piece of a highly aligned message around our *Inspiring Purpose.*

Another great example of an organization with a highly motivating daily purpose is Boom Supersonic. Based out of Denver, on June 17, 2024, Boom Supersonic completed construction of the first supersonic airliner factory in the United States. They are committed to "make the world dramatically more accessible through a return to supersonic passenger travel that is more affordable, more convenient, and more sustainable."

The goals for Boom Supersonic's flagship aircraft, Overture, which already had secured 130 preorders by mid-2024, include flying 20 percent faster over land than conventional aircraft and at an altitude of 60,000 feet, which is well above the jet stream that often slows westbound flights by as much as 100 knots. They also have design projections that will allow the Overture to cruise at Mach 1.7 over water, which is two times faster than conventional aircraft. This means that a flight from Atlanta to Madrid or from New York to Rome, which both take approximately eight hours today, can be made in just four and a half hours in the Overture.[16]

All of the innovation that is going into Boom Supersonic requires new ways of thinking in terms of avionics, flight deck design, and the use of an augmented reality vision system so they don't need to require a lowering nose cone for takeoff and landing, like with the Concorde design. They've designed an evolved turbofan engine, the Symphony, which will be assembled by StandardAero in San Antonio and is being purpose-built for supersonic flight.

For anyone who is in the aerospace industry, from executives to designers, engineers, test pilots, and mechanics, the purpose behind Boom Supersonic is one of inspiration, imagination, and creativity that allows Boom to attract the best of the best talent from around the world. Much like Apple under Steve Jobs, the purpose, or why, behind the organization attracts people who believe in that purpose and who want to be part of its advancement.

> "It's not just about telling people what you want to tell them, but clearly communicating and explaining the why behind it. The more a person understands the purpose and the why behind what you do, the more they want to follow you. When you do this, what seems otherwise like an artificial and pedestrian reason to do something all of a sudden has great meaning."[17]
>
> —DR. NIDO QUBEIN

---

16 Boom, "Accelerating Towards Supersonic," Boom Supersonic, accessed December 5, 2024, https://boomsupersonic.com/.

17 Nido Qubein, interview by the author, October 14, 2024.

HOW TO DESCRIBE YOUR WHY

Most organizations haven't done a particularly good job of articulating what they stand for—their "mission statements" notwithstanding. Some of them don't stand for anything real and truly are just a means to make money. Other organizations that do stand for something simply don't have a good grasp of what it is. So, back to the question at the start of this section:

- If you're the founder, why did you start the business, beyond making money? What were you feeling at the time that you started it, and what did you want to do in service of the marketplace?
- If you're a leader in an organization without a clear purpose, why did you join the company? Beyond money, what first attracted you to the organization? Why, beyond money, do you choose to stay? What is it about the work you do and the outcomes you accomplish that brings you joy and keeps you committed to the organization?

Somewhere in the answers to the questions above lies your purpose—your "why."

There are five important characteristics of a good expression of an organization's daily purpose:

1. It has to be inspiring to people inside the company.
2. It has to be something that will be as valid one hundred years from now as it is today.
3. It should help you think expansively and creatively about what you could be doing but are not currently doing.
4. It should make clear what opportunities and ideas you should avoid.

5. It must be truly authentic to the organization and what it stands for.

It is also important to remember that words matter, and it is worth taking your time to think this through and get it right. In my conversation with Nido as I was working on this book, I asked him to share his insights on the importance of using the right words to inspire people:

> I did all kinds of crazy things. For example, I changed all the words we were using for our teams at High Point University. We rebranded our food service department as our hospitality team. By using different terms and words, people began to behave differently. If you think you are in food service, you just worry about making the food. If you are in hospitality service, you are hosting guests in your restaurant, and that's a different mindset.
>
> We stopped using the term "maintenance department" and instead began to use the phrase "campus enhancement team." If you think you are in maintenance, your focus is on ensuring things are working, but if you're in campus enhancement, you are focused not only on the functionality of things but also on how they look. That leads to more beauty on the campus as a result of people taking more pride in their work because they are not just fixing broken things; they are enhancing everything.
>
> While this may sound like I'm just playing with words, that person cooking the food, when they know their job is not just about food service but hospitality, or the engineer who thinks of themselves as part of the campus enhancement team, wow…they approach their job very differently.[18]

One of our clients, Coxreels®, has been in business for over one hundred years and manufactures reels for the safe and efficient management of hoses, cords, and cables. While not exactly a commodity, they are constantly competing against cheap imports. This type of business

---

18 Nido Qubein, interview by the author, October 14, 2024.

often requires more thought and work to truly unpack and understand a statement of why the organization exists that can be used to inspire people to see beyond the product that they make. It is much easier if you happen to be in a business that is changing the world.

When working with their Next Level Growth Partner and Business Guide, the Coxreels leadership team was asked the questions described earlier and also asked to explain it in a way that did not speak to the product they manufacture, just to what they do that is of value and service to the marketplace. The product is covered in the strategic niche.

After several rounds of dialogue and seeing different words and phrases on the whiteboard, it started to come together. When viewed through the lens of their daily purpose alone, Coxreels exists *to help people work smarter, not harder, by bringing passionate innovation to solving problems.*

By being very aware of their daily purpose, and in a never-ending, relentless effort to execute it to a very high standard, Coxreels can begin to frame the way people think about their jobs and approach problems and opportunities. Think about it through the lens of the five statements about a daily purpose.

1. *It has to be inspiring to people inside the company.* Even for an assembly worker in a tough manufacturing environment, this understanding of a daily purpose is about more than just an eight-hour job; it is about thinking creatively and solving problems; it is about working smarter, not harder. That applies both externally and internally. It invites front-line employees into problem-solving and inspires them to be part of solutions to overcoming challenges.
2. *It has to be something that could be as valid one hundred years from now as it is today.* The key concepts of working

smarter, not harder, and bringing passionate innovation to problem-solving are not a time-bound purpose. This statement would have been impactful one hundred years ago and it is difficult to imagine a time when these things would not be important and impactful.

3. *It should help you think expansively and creatively about what you could be doing but are not currently doing.* A focus on this daily purpose invites creative and innovative thinking. It requires them to know and understand their customers and analyze together the ways to make work easier.

4. *It should make it clear what opportunities and ideas you should avoid.* This daily purpose frames things through a lens of the Return on Investment they can create through adding value, which means that while they will always focus on efficient use of resources, being cheap to save costs just to compete on price will never be part of their focus. Opportunities to lower costs by using substandard materials will be opportunities they will not consider.

5. *It must be truly authentic to the organization and what it stands for.* James Cox founded Coxreels in 1923 with a vision of providing a better service station experience for attendants and customers. He did this through his innovative creation of a reel system to manage air, water, and fuel hoses. If you're old enough to remember the days when air hoses at gas stations were stored underground and only the top of the hose was exposed, you're old enough to have seen firsthand the original idea that was the birth of Coxreels.

In 2019, ten years after publishing *Start with Why*, Sinek published *The Infinite Game*, which memorializes an evolution of Sinek's thoughts about building organizations for the long term. In this book, he introduced the idea of a Just Cause. As we began to understand and discuss the concept at Next Level Growth, our team of Guides saw Just Cause as a key and missing piece to telling an inspiring story and one that would elevate Jim Collins's hedgehog concept into what we call an *Inspiring Purpose*.

JUST CAUSE

Simon Sinek describes a Just Cause as a "specific vision of a future state that does not yet exist; a future state so appealing that people are willing to make sacrifices in order to help advance toward that vision." He goes on to say, "A Just Cause is not the same as our Why."

> A "why" comes from the past. It is an origin story... A Just Cause is about the future and defines where we are going. It describes the world we hope to live in and will commit to help build.[19]

To summarize, a Just Cause is a core belief around which an organization is built, and often starts with a phrase like, "We envision a world where...," or "We believe that..." One thing that is important to us all at Next Level Growth is to test things on ourselves before we take them to our clients, so with this new concept in front of me, I set out to uncover my own Just Cause and determine how to link it back to the bigger story behind Next Level Growth and why it is much more than just a business to me.

In my 2017 memoir, *RISE: The Reincarnation of an Entrepreneur*—a book about which former COO of 1-800-GOT-JUNK? Cameron Herold says, "I've met countless entrepreneurs...few have stories as dramatic—and in the end as inspirational—as Michael Erath's"—I share the highs and lows of my own entrepreneurial journey with great

---

19 Simon Sinek, *The Infinite Game* (Portfolio/Penguin, 2019), 33.

vulnerability and transparency.[20] My story is one of incredible highs and extremely dark lows. As I mentioned earlier, during the first half of my career, I spent seven years as a member of YPO and another seven years as a member of EO. From both my own career as well as my time getting to know countless other entrepreneurs, one thing became clear to me:

> *Most entrepreneurial leaders achieve success,*
> *to some degree, at the expense of their*
> *relationships, their time with family, their*
> *physical health, or their emotional health.*
> *Oftentimes, all four areas suffer.*

For all the risks that entrepreneurs take, and all they provide to our world and our communities through innovation, job creation, and improved lives, it just doesn't seem right. That is almost always what is at the core of understanding your Just Cause, a passion to overcome an injustice, unfairness, or something you believe can be better than the status quo. When you think about your beliefs and how they relate to and influence your *why*, your Just Cause will start to become clear. To me, it had to do with everything entrepreneurs sacrifice in hopes of earning a return on their investment and how, for many, it robs them of their Return on Life. After spending some time reflecting on everything the first half of my career had shown me and thinking about the work that we were doing at Next Level Growth, it became clear to me. Starting with the phrase, "We believe," I finally arrived at our Just Cause.

> *We believe entrepreneurial leaders deserve*
> *more than a Return on Investment, they*
> *deserve a meaningful Return on Life.*

---

20 Michael Erath, *RISE: The Reincarnation of an Entrepreneur* (Lioncrest Publishing, 2017), 15.

While the thought that one day every entrepreneur will experience a meaningful Return on Life is not likely, a Just Cause is about a belief you hold so strongly that you will commit your career toward its advancement. We firmly believe that Next Level Growth has the opportunity to have a significant impact in advancing this Just Cause through at least the organizations we are able to work with and help. In fact, that is at the core of why I decided to write this book and essentially give away so much of the content that we have spent years curating and refining. With an abundance mindset, we genuinely want to help as many people as we possibly can. At the end of the day, it is the successes that our clients experience on their journey to what we like to call "entrepreneurial freedom." Sharing those success stories among ourselves as a team of elite Business Guides motivates and inspires us to do more, to dream bigger, and to push ourselves to learn, grow, and evolve.

Connecting the dots between your Just Cause and your Daily Purpose in a clear way is very important internally to keep people focused on how they need to show up every day and what, at the end of the day, matters most. When we put these two statements together, we have the foundation of our *Inspiring Purpose*:

> *We believe entrepreneurial leaders deserve more than a Return on Investment, they deserve to earn a meaningful Return on Life. This belief drives our Daily Purpose of Helping Entrepreneurial Leaders Build Elite Organizations.*

When we fully understand the interplay between these two statements, and when we both celebrate the wins we accomplish and use the failures as feedback from which we can learn and grow, we have a unifying and common focus that motivates our decisions and actions on a daily basis.

If we go back to our example with Coxreels, they were asked by their Guide to go through the same thought process and work on the same kind of statement. Fortunately, the Cox family and the Coxreels organization have done an excellent job at preserving the history and the stories of the business over the years, so third-generation CEO Brad Cox was able to articulate his answers well.

Imagine life in 1923. It was only thirty-eight years since 1885, when Carl Benz had developed the gasoline-powered automobile, and thirty years since the first gasoline-powered automobile had been sold in the United States, a one-cylinder, four-horsepower Duryea. Filling stations, as they were called at the time, were still in the early stages of development, and the equipment was very rudimentary. Air, water, and fuel hoses, which were made primarily from rubber or early forms of synthetic material, were not as robust as modern hoses and were prone to wear, cracking, and leakage over time. This was accelerated by exposure to the elements and the manual nature of how they had to be handled.

Before the invention of hose reels, managing and storing hoses at gas stations and other facilities were relatively simple but labor-intensive tasks. The most common method of managing hoses was manually coiling them after each use. In many cases, hoses were simply coiled and left on the ground near the pump or equipment. This was the least ideal method, as it exposed the hose to dirt, potential damage from vehicles, and wear from being stepped on. In addition to the safety hazards of a leaking hose, it also posed a tripping hazard. This was something that James Cox saw as an unnecessary danger and was the driving force behind his initial designs for reliable, underground hose reels that would improve storage and safety at filling stations. With hoses neatly stored and quickly retractable, the risk of tripping hazards and unnecessary wear and damage was reduced, and the overall speed of service was increased. This was particularly important as the number of vehicles and demand for air, water, and fuel services continued to rise.

As the team discussed the history of the organization and talked about the beliefs that drive their daily purpose and have since the founding of the company, their Just Cause came into focus, and when coupled with their Daily Purpose, is now stated as follows:

> *At Coxreels, we believe that the people who*
> *get things done deserve to get them done*
> *safely, productively, and with less fatigue.*
> *This belief drives our Daily Purpose of*
> *helping people work smarter, not harder,*
> *by bringing passionate innovation to*
> *solving problems.*

Sometimes, organizations will do really great work in an off site meeting and come up with similar statements through similar means. But none of this is of any value if you don't execute on it. At Coxreels, as with the companies we work with, and at Next Level Growth as well, the Just Cause and Daily Purpose are talked about frequently. The more people hear it, and the more stories are shared with team members about things that are happening week in and week out to fulfill the organization's Daily Purpose and advance its Just Cause, the more real it becomes to them. When your organization is filled with people who understand and embrace your Just Cause and Daily Purpose, and they can see how their role contributes to this bigger idea and belief, the more passion, creativity, and energy they will bring to their work and the more engaged your people will be.

STRATEGIC NICHE

In Jim Collins's hedgehog concept, he refers to an organization's strategic niche as "what you can be the best in the world at."[21] While Collins was researching large, publicly traded companies that perhaps could be the best in the world, most entrepreneurial organizations likely won't achieve "best in the world" status. In our experience, when that is the underlying question an entrepreneur is faced with in clarifying their strategic niche, they often struggle. For that reason, we prefer to use an adaptation of Michael Porter's definition of a strategic niche: *At what can you provide consistent, differentiated value in the marketplace?* When this answer becomes clear, and when you can show how it advances your Just Cause, it drives an incredibly powerful focus.

Notice that I specifically use the term *Strategic Niche* and not just *niche*. If you focus only on your niche, you just talk about your product in a homogenous way. For example, at Next Level Growth, our niche alone would simply be described as a "Business Operating and Scaling System." That's no different than anyone else in our industry and does not speak to our strategic differentiation. Coxreels' niche is simply "Reels for managing hoses, cords, and cables." No different than all of the cheap imports in the marketplace.

What makes a strategic niche different is the inclusion of words or phrases that speak to Porter's question about how your organization can provide consistent, differentiated value in the marketplace. To satisfy a strategic niche and to complete the way you frame your *Inspiring Purpose*, you must be clear on how you accomplish all three things: You must be able to execute your strategic niche consistently and be differentiated from your competition in some way, and the market must see and appreciate the value in the differentiation.

---

21 Collins, "The Hedgehog Concept."

Strategic Niche—A Few Examples

When we look at our own business and survey the landscape of what exists in the world of business coaching and business operating systems, the default is toward "one-size-fits-all" systems. While these systems often provide value for smaller companies and entrepreneurs who don't have any systems or structures, they are usually more about the system than the user. Since breaking away from EOS and Scaling Up, we've talked to hundreds of entrepreneurs who feel that the business operating systems they have tried are too rigid, or the business coaches they worked with were trying to force fit them into a system rather than making the system fit their unique organizations.

We've also noticed that many business operating systems have a relatively low bar for allowing people to become coaches within their system, and we think this is what drives their insistence on purity and a one-size-fits-all approach. As mentioned earlier in this book, at Next Level Growth, we only allow people who have been owners, CEOs, or presidents of businesses with at least ten million in revenue and fifty or more employees to apply to become a Partner and Business Guide. This is a key component of our own strategic niche because a significant level of real-world experience allows every one of our Business Guides to take a freestyle approach in working with their clients whenever it becomes necessary to achieve a desired outcome, and it protects our brand. Less capable coaches don't have the experience to be highly flexible and meet clients where they are. They have to have a rigid system and structure, with well-defined guardrails, to fall back on. This also speaks to the scale of businesses we are able to work with and provide value for. As of 2025, our smallest client is a three-million-dollar professional services firm and our largest is a construction company nearing one billion in annual revenue.

To stand out and be different, we have formed our strategic niche around flipping this common frustration with business operating systems on its head. At Next Level Growth, our Strategic Niche is "*A principled, individualized, outcomes-based approach to customizable Business Operating & Scaling System implementation & ongoing guidance to the Summit.*"

Remember, a Strategic Niche should clearly define how you provide *consistent, differentiated, and appreciated value* in the marketplace. For us, there are four key differentiators.

1. *Providing an individualized approach.* To do this, we spend time in the discovery process getting to know and understand a potential client's business, their ownership structure, and the unique challenges they face. We will often pair them with a Next Level Growth Partner and Business Guide who has experience either in the same industry or in a near-similar industry so that we can provide more unique insights and guidance.

2. *Taking an outcomes-based approach.* While we have recommendations of best practices and offer key foundational concepts, not all tools and concepts work in all cases. If something we teach a client isn't working for them, we seek out alternative solutions and work with them to achieve the outcome, not reteach the same tool or concept and hope they will get a different outcome. We also challenge our clients to be accountable and do the work. If, over time, we feel that a client is not as committed to their own success as we are and that they are not doing the work, we will call the end of an engagement and free up our capacity to work with someone who will be more committed and accountable. In my ten years as a Business Guide, I have personally fired a handful of clients simply because they were not willing to

do the work and were satisfied with being average to good rather than excellent or elite.

3. *Focusing on customizations.* As a result of our outcomes-based approach, our clients do end up with a business operating system, but one that is custom-tailored to them and their unique needs and circumstances. It is about them, not us, about the user, not the system. Everything fits better when it is custom-tailored.

4. *Requiring the right experience.* Because of our own experiences scaling our own businesses, for the clients who want us to remain roped in with them long-term, we are equipped to grow and evolve with them, continuing to provide significant value to them much longer than a typical business coach who can only teach them a certain set of tools and then runs out of value to add. As a testament to this, we have clients who are now in their tenth consecutive year of working with a Next Level Growth Business Guide, and we've only been in business for ten years. Because we don't have contracts or require prepayments, if we were not providing significant ongoing and evolving value, they would not be staying with us.

Going back to our Coxreels example, they are focused on producing a higher quality, durable reel that puts them in a premium category. They do this because of their belief in safety and efficiency, so the way they articulate their Strategic Niche is:

> *Reels for the safe and efficient management of hoses, cords, and cables.*

INSPIRING PURPOSE— PULLING IT ALL TOGETHER

When you put all three elements together, you have a statement that clarifies what you believe as an organization, how that belief guides you on a daily basis, and the specific, unique way that you will advance your *Inspiring Purpose*. You have something that both your internal and external stakeholders can relate to and embrace that will help you on your relentless journey to building an elite organization.

Our friends at Coxreels continue to climb their business mountain because:

> At Coxreels, we believe that the people who get things done deserve to get them done safely, productively, and with less fatigue. This belief drives our Daily Purpose of helping people work smarter, not harder, by bringing passionate innovation to solving problems and we accomplish this through the manufacture and distribution of reels for the safe and efficient management of hoses, cords, and cables.

When we pull together the same elements of the entire *Inspiring Purpose* at Next Level Growth, what we like to refer to as "Why we climb," we have the statement:

> We believe entrepreneurial leaders deserve more than a Return on Investment, they deserve to earn a meaningful Return on Life. This belief drives our Daily Purpose of Helping Entrepreneurial Leaders Build Elite Organizations and we accomplish this through providing a principled, individualized, outcomes-based approach to customizable Business Operating and Scaling System implementation and ongoing guidance to the Summit.

This short paragraph defines the foundation of our unique business model and value proposition. For those who are the right fit to be part of our organization, whether as a team member or a client, it provides inspiration and speaks to the essence of what incites passion in us all.

INCORPORATING THE FLYWHEEL AND SMAC RECIPE TO PULL IT ALL TOGETHER

When we view our business as a flywheel, another concept from Collins's *Good to Great*, at Next Level Growth, there are seven key components, each which builds on the one before and provides a clear and simplified overview of our business model. Here is the Next Level Growth flywheel as an example.

Figure 4.1

This simple, visual representation of our business model provides something that, when shared with team members, offers an easy way to understand our business model and how we are unique. We also keep it close at hand to review when faced with strategic decisions. At Next Level Growth, as long as we make sure that all of our strategies and plans are aligned with our flywheel, and our team members are making decisions through the lens of our flywheel, we stay focused on making the right decisions and leveraging the right strategies to effectively continue to scale the business over time. If you have not thought through and created your own flywheel, please consider investing the time and effort, as it is well worth it. If you get stuck, consider reaching out to one of our Partners and Business Guides through our website.

While I only provided an overview of the SMaC Recipe concept earlier in this chapter, consider reading more about it in *Great by Choice* and working on your own Specific, Methodical, and Consistent recipe. Here is the copy of our SMaC Recipe, which can be found on the wall just inside the doors of our Phoenix headquarters where every client can see it and help hold us accountable to living it out every day:

To advance our Just Cause and Daily Purpose, we are fiercely committed to living out our SMaC Recipe:

1. We will always put our clients' needs first and treat them as our number one priority.
2. We will never put any system, or purity to any tool or concept, over the client's needs.
3. We will only engage with highly experienced former owners, CEOs, and presidents to serve as our Business

Guides, maintaining a focus on our one-phrase strategy, "Experience Matters."

4. We will always maintain a safe and confidential space for our clients to open up and share anything they need to share in order to build healthier, stronger teams and organizations.

5. We will always provide a fun environment and maintain a sense of humor in our work together.

6. We will obsess about and invest in creating outstanding experiences for our clients.

7. We will obsess about learning and growing our skills as Business Guides—we will never settle or stagnate.

8. We will obsess about our clients' results and the experience they are having with Next Level Growth.

9. We will provide an ecosystem for our clients to connect, learn, and grow together.

10. We will support our Business Guides in their professional development, and we will always be there for each other because the more we help each other, the more we can help our clients and advance our Just Cause.

As we make strategic decisions, we always weigh them against this *Inspiring Purpose*, our flywheel, and our SMaC Recipe. We ask ourselves, "If we choose A versus B, or if we move forward with something or choose not to, will it accelerate our momentum toward advancing our *Inspiring Purpose*? Will it accelerate or work against our flywheel? Will it violate our SMaC Recipe? Or might it distract us and cause us to dilute our focus?" These questions, viewed through these various lenses, help us to protect ourselves against chasing shiny objects or opportunities that are not aligned with our long-term strategy and vision.

Please don't overlook the importance of an *Inspiring Purpose* for your organization. Follow the steps laid out in this chapter to discover and wordsmith your own. And with *Great People*, aligned around and motivated by an *Inspiring Purpose*, you need to equip them with *Optimized Playbooks*, the third of the Five Obsessions of Elite Organizations.

Chapter 5

OBSESSION #3: OPTIMIZED PLAYBOOKS

> "Organize around business functions, not people. Build systems within each business function. Let systems run the business and people run the systems. People come and go but the systems remain constant."
>
> —MICHAEL E. GERBER, *The E-Myth Revisited*

Evan was excited as he pulled into the parking lot early on the first day of his new job. He had been hired as a field supervisor for a growing construction company after several years of working as a technician in different roles for a subcontracting company in the same town. As he parked his car and made his way toward the office, he smiled with pride for this next big, exciting step in his young career. He was twenty-seven years old.

When he entered the office, he was greeted by Debbie, whom he had met during his interviews. Debbie was in the accounting department and also took care of getting new employees set up on payroll and benefits and otherwise oriented into the company. As Evan was sitting in the office filling out a few of the initial forms Debbie needed from him, Lee, one of the project managers who interviewed him, came hurriedly out of his office and looked at Evan. "Let's go! You can fill that out later. We've got an issue on one of the projects you're going to be supervising, and you might as well start out by jumping into the fire with me."

Evan and Lee walked out, jumped in Lee's truck, and raced out of the parking lot.

Lee was a seasoned project manager with a reputation for getting things done by sheer force of will. As they drove to the jobsite, Lee briefed Evan on the project. The company was renovating an old office building, transforming it into modern retail spaces on the street level with condominiums above. The job was behind schedule, and tensions were high.

They pulled up to the site, and Evan immediately sensed something was off. The air was thick with a pungent, acrid smell that made his nose wrinkle. As they approached the building, they saw smoke lingering in the air, and the unmistakable blackened edges of a fuse panel greeted them at the entrance.

"Damn it," Lee muttered under his breath, picking up the pace. Evan hurried after him, his heart pounding. Inside, a group of workers stood around, their faces etched with worry and frustration. A section of the wall was charred, and the smell of burnt plastic and wiring was overwhelming.

"What happened here?" Lee demanded, his voice sharp.

One of the electricians, an older man with soot-streaked hands, stepped forward. "It was the new kid Joey, the apprentice. He was supposed to service the HVAC unit in the mechanical room and needed to replace the blower motor. But he didn't pull the fuse from the fuse panel before he started working. When he tried to disconnect the wires, the whole thing sparked and caught fire."

Lee cursed under his breath and turned to Evan. "Why the hell people do things like this is beyond me. That kid shouldn't have been doing anything without someone checking his work first."

Evan nodded, taking in the scene. The apprentice, a young man barely out of his teens, stood off to the side, looking shell-shocked. His hands were shaking, and he kept staring at the damage as if willing it to disappear.

"Does anyone know if there's a checklist or a process for electrical work or supervising an apprentice?" Evan asked, trying to gather some information.

The older electrician shook his head and laughed. "Nope. We've been doing things by the seat of our pants around here for as long as I can remember. Everyone just follows what the guy before him did."

Lee chimed in, "Can't you see how busy we are? Who has time to sit down and write a bunch of manuals on how to do your job when people need to just use their brains and know how to do their job? Let's get this mess cleaned up and hope this doesn't delay us even more."

Evan frowned. He had expected that there would be some sort of logical approach to his training and onboarding as a supervisor, but he was beginning to sense that was not going to be the case. As a first-time leader, he also began to wonder if this kind of chaos was actually pretty common and questioned how he could be successful as a leader in an organization that didn't have basic processes and good training in place.

Over the days that followed, the chaos continued. Every day a different problem, but always as a result of a lack of systems, processes, and effective onboarding and training.

Fast-forward twenty years, and Evan now owns his own electrical contracting business, primarily working as a subcontractor in the commercial construction industry. He shared this story with me over breakfast one morning when we were talking about common mistakes organizations make when they bring in new employees or when they promote existing employees into leadership positions for the first time. Evan's story highlights a very common problem that limits the growth and value of entrepreneurial organizations: a lack of Process Playbooks to systemize how they do things and supporting checklists for team members on the front lines to help ensure they don't accidentally miss a crucial step in a process, as the apprentice did in Evan's story, causing an electrical fire that could have been much, much worse.

The problem is that many leaders in entrepreneurial organizations either discount the value of Process Playbooks relative to the work required to create and properly utilize them, or they procrastinate putting time into working on them, and as a result, they never get done. In my experience, they do this for one of the following reasons:

- They confuse "Process Playbooks" with detailed work instructions or SOP (Standard Operating Procedure) manuals, which are usually hundreds if not thousands of pages and almost never utilized due to their sheer volume and complexity.
- They claim to already have documented processes, but when pressed, admit that they are scattered across multiple locations, not easy to find, and not arranged in a comprehensive manner.
- They recognize that they don't have their processes

documented and argue that they are too busy "firefighting" to spend time documenting processes.

When it comes to confusing Process Playbooks with more detailed and much larger books and manuals, I often find this objection coming from people who have, at some point in their career, worked in larger or publicly traded organizations. Many times, these larger organizations have either built documentation required to earn an ISO (International Standards Organization) designation or were otherwise required to build out massive documentation on how every job scenario was to be performed. Due to their ultimate volume and complexity, these documents were rarely referenced and used by employees once they were put in place and the desired certifications were achieved.

Think of a high-level Process Playbook as the "roadmap" for a journey to complete an operation within an organization. It outlines the starting point, the destination, the ideal route, major milestones, and key sub-steps, providing a clear overview of the overall objectives and basic steps to complete the objective consistently every time. It helps guide decision-making and keeps everyone aligned with the big picture. In contrast, detailed work instructions or SOPs are like the "turn-by-turn directions" within that roadmap. They provide specific, step-by-step instructions on how to carry out each task, ensuring consistency, precision, and compliance with established standards. While the SOPs focus on the exact procedures needed to accomplish each part of the process, the playbook offers a broader context and strategic framework.

As an example, at Next Level Growth, we have a Process Playbook for what needs to happen when we get a new prospect. That process has just thirteen steps. That's it. Those steps are written based on the assumption that our team members have been appropriately trained on how to execute each step, so the playbook simply serves as a reminder of the necessary steps from start to finish that must be done every time in order to ensure that we have both captured everything we need and stored it in the right place, and also that the new lead has the kind of on-brand experience that we want them to have every time.

One of those steps along the way is "Create a new lead in CRM." If an admin team member has been trained on how to create a new lead in our CRM, they know what to do to complete that step. The difference between this "playbook step" and a more detailed work instruction is that the detailed work instruction would include every step involved in how to create a new lead in the CRM, how to navigate through the menu function of the CRM, and what buttons to click on each screen. In a work instruction document, that one playbook step could turn into two to three pages of highly detailed instructions that walk through, step by step, what a new employee might need to learn during their onboarding and initial training.

Speaking of onboarding and initial training and how that does require some form of work instructions, something we do at Next Level Growth to simplify the creation of these onboarding work instructions is to use video instead of written documentation. Almost everything can be learned through a video, whether it is a video of somebody doing something or a screen recording of how to navigate a software product to complete a task. Within our Process Playbooks, new team members have the ability to drill down into videos to show them how to properly complete a step in our higher-level processes.

Taking this approach creates value in several ways. First, the steps a new team member needs to be trained on are steps that are already being done by experienced people, so to create the video work instructions, you just need to record somebody doing something they already have to do. For example, as we were building ours, I simply asked my executive assistant, the next time she was adding a new lead to our

CRM, to create a screen share video of her completing the task and record herself talking through it as though she was teaching a new hire who had never used our CRM before. This did not require her to waste time creating a "mock" scenario for training purposes; she just recorded something she had to do anyway. Also, when a new assistant comes on board, rather than one of our existing team members needing to spend hours training and onboarding the new hire, there is a library of video training aligned with our Process Playbooks for them to watch. The first few times a new admin is adding a lead to our CRM, they just watch the video and follow along. After a few repetitions, they won't need the video anymore, and they're up to speed without taking lots of hours from existing team members to teach them all the steps.

To be effective, Process Playbooks need to be housed in a logical fashion and in a repository that is easy to access and use. The effectiveness of any onboarding and training system is very dependent on its effective utility and ease of use. You cannot expect people to be well trained when the system you provide them for onboarding and training is a total mess. We have seen effective Process Playbook repositories in things as simple as documents in Microsoft Word, with hyperlinks to external manuals and videos containing the work instructions, simple and effective training platforms, and complex full-featured Learning Management Systems (LMS). As is true for almost all things process-related, don't overcomplicate it. Simple and clear is a great place to start.

If you would like an introduction to one of the more common LMS systems used by our clients, just visit NextLevelGrowth.com and click on "Start a Conversation." Make sure to include in the message field that you're looking for a LMS Recommendation.

The irony of the most common objection, the one about being too busy firefighting to create process documentation, is that most of the fires we fight as leaders in entrepreneurial organizations wouldn't happen if we had well-defined, consistently followed processes in place. When I hear this objection, it is almost always a situation of being too busy and distracted to do the very thing that would prevent you from being too busy and distracted.

Reflecting back on the quote widely attributed to Paul Batalden and noted at the beginning of Chapter 1—"Every system is perfectly designed to get the results it gets"—I would ask you to look within your own organization. Where are your greatest frustrations and pain points? What are your customer's or client's most common complaints or frustrations? Use that as a starting point to explore where the opportunities exist to begin optimizing your Process Playbooks.

THE ROOT CAUSE OF ALMOST ALL
YOUR BUSINESS ISSUES

Over the course of my career, it has become very clear to me that the root cause of almost all issues in business is either one of people or process and if you don't have optimized Process Playbooks for people to train on and follow, you cannot always be certain that people are your problem.

Whenever we are talking with entrepreneurs or leaders in entrepreneurial businesses about their frustrations within the organization, something regarding people is almost always mentioned. However, as we unpack with them why that is the case, we typically reach a point where they have a broken or missing process that is the real cause of the frustration they are feeling with their people. Harvey Mackay, founder of MackayMitchell Envelope Company, author, and professional speaker, likes to say that "agreements prevent disagreements."[22] Process Playbooks, coupled with a strong onboarding and initial training system, help to create agreements between new team members and their leaders as to how things are expected to be done…and the clearer those agreements, the less likely you are to have future disagreements.

ONBOARDING OR WATERBOARDING?

Whenever we ask leaders in organizations if they have a great and consistent onboarding process for new employees or if new team members tend to get waterboarded, with a bit of a guilty chuckle, they almost always admit to some degree of waterboarding their new team members.

They expect people to come into their organizations and perform, but they don't bring them on board through a great, well-thought-out process and train them on *Optimized Playbooks* for their role. Instead of being well-onboarded into an organization and a job, most employees get tossed into the deep end of the pool too quickly and without sufficient preparation, just like Evan and the apprentice in the opening story of this chapter. Excellence is often the expectation in terms of outcomes, but systems are more often designed for mediocrity at best. As a result, employees suffer, their teams suffer, their leaders suffer, the company suffers, and in the end, the customer suffers.

Employees Suffer

When we fail to properly and sufficiently onboard and train new team members, those new employees quickly go from a place of being excited about their new job to being frustrated after they are

---

22 Mackay, "70 Years of Brutally Honest Business Advice."

launched into a role where they often don't fully know what to do. They risk either getting in trouble for doing something wrong or they have to constantly interrupt their colleagues to get help and ongoing instruction.

This has a negative impact on their ability to build relationships within their team and ultimately creates a sense of frustration in the way they perceive their leader and the organization. As a result, they either live in fight-or-flight mode, making it harder for them to focus and perform, or worse, they become apathetic and no longer care about the organization that they feel abandoned them.

Teams Suffer

When a new team is formed, and this also happens to some degree every time a new team member joins a team, there is a four-stage, natural process that takes place. This phenomenon was first introduced in 1965 by psychologist Bruce Tuckman. He proposed the model as a way to describe the stages of team development and dynamics he was observing. According to Tuckman, each of these stages is essential for a team to grow, face challenges, tackle problems, find solutions, plan work, and deliver results. By understanding the characteristics and strategies to accelerate through each stage, teams can get to the final performing stage much faster and with minimal collateral damage. Having a well-designed onboarding playbook will accelerate the velocity through this process.

Here is a brief overview of each stage:

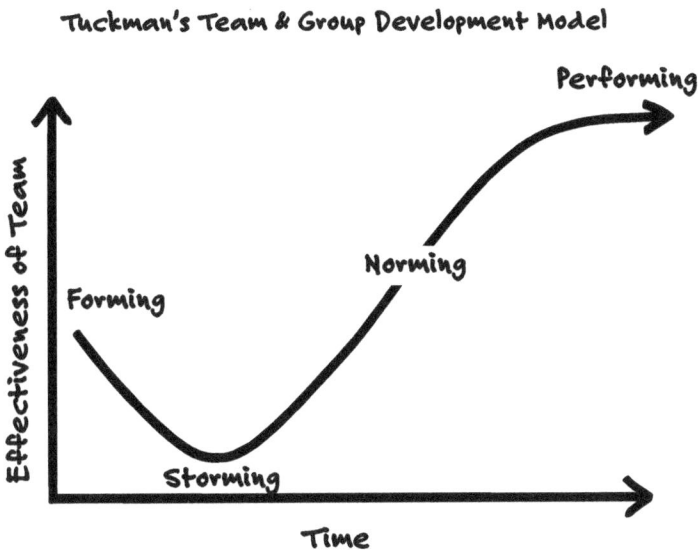

Figure 5.1

Forming: Characteristics of Forming include displaying eagerness, socializing with colleagues, using a generally polite tone with one another, sticking to safe topics, coupled with feeling unclear about how to fit in, together with some anxiety and questioning.

Leadership strategies for moving quickly through this phase include leaders truly taking the lead, being highly visible, facilitating introductions, clarifying the big picture for how the team works together, establishing clear expectations, communicating success criteria, and ensuring that response times are quick.

Without a well-designed onboarding and training system in place, most teams, and most new hires, get stuck in the trough between Forming, Storming, and Norming for far too long, negatively affecting the overall performance of the team.

Storming: Traits of Storming include resistance, lack of participation, conflict related to differences of feelings and opinions, competition, high emotions, and eventually starting to move toward group norms.

Leadership strategies for moving quickly through this phase include requesting and encouraging feedback, identifying issues and facilitating their resolution, normalizing matters for the team, and building trust by honoring commitments.

Norming: Norming includes an improved sense of purpose and understanding of goals, higher confidence, improved commitment, team members becoming engaged and supportive, lowered anxiety, and a sense of cohesion beginning to form throughout the team.

Leadership strategies for moving quickly through this phase include recognizing individual and team efforts, providing opportunities for learning and feedback, and monitoring the energy of the team.

Performing: As teams move into the ideal state, the Performing stage, you will begin to see signs of higher motivation, elevated trust and empathy, individuals typically deferring to the team's needs over their own interests and agendas, effective production, consistent performance, and demonstrations of interdependence and self-management.

Leadership strategies for maintaining this phase include "guiding from the side" (minimal intervention), celebrating successes, and encouraging collective decision-making and problem-solving.

Tuckman's model has become a foundational concept in understanding group dynamics and is widely used in organizational development, project management, and leadership training. A well-designed onboarding system, with capable team leaders in place, is essential to ensure that teams don't suffer unnecessary challenges when new team members are brought on board.

Leaders Suffer

When we fail to properly and sufficiently onboard and train new team members, we inadvertently take our leaders' focus, which should be looking forward, or as Jocko Willink says, "up and out," while the team executes its work, and instead direct their attention "down and in," micromanaging and firefighting as a result of poorly onboarded team members.

When leaders are focused "down and in," they do not see the potential coming problems or opportunities because their focus is not where it needs to be for them to serve their highest and greatest use and bring the most value. They also become frustrated from feeling like they are too deep in the weeds. The more frustrated the leader becomes, the less effective they will be.

The Company Suffers

When new employees struggle to reach the expected levels of proficiency and performance in their roles within a reasonable time frame, entire teams suffer as a result. Couple that with team leaders who are too in the weeds to be focused on the areas where they bring the greatest value, and it is only natural that the company suffers. The disruptions of poorly onboarded team members often lead to reduced efficiency and an increase in errors and mistakes. Those things then lead to reduced margins and decreased financial performance.

Companies under undue financial stress often become very reactive and take their eye off the culture they want to have. As a result, the culture begins to erode or never reaches its desired potential in the first place. The frustrations become widespread up and down the organizational structure, and this destructive cycle gains momentum. Chaos becomes the norm.

The Customer Suffers

Ultimately, and tragically, the customer suffers, and when the customer suffers, the organization has a problem that is bigger and takes longer to correct. Your customers, or clients, have choices in the marketplace, and when customers are on the receiving end of inconsistencies from their vendors, it typically doesn't take them very long to make a change and move to a new vendor.

As customer attrition grows, the organization's reputation in the marketplace begins to suffer, and while building a good reputation in the market is a long journey of consistency and hard work, a bad reputation can come about in a matter of just weeks or months. Winning new business often takes time for many organizations and is not an inexpensive process. Winning back lost business is even more time-consuming and costly.

ONBOARDING PROCESSES— STARTING POINT

A simple solution and starting point that we teach all of our clients at Next Level Growth for an onboarding process requires alignment around two things: frequency and content. The reason our recommendation is so widely accepted and utilized is that it is simple and universal to every role in the organization. However, to be effective, you must have in place authentic behavioral core values and a Next Level Accountability Chart, complete with a clear Mission, Most Critical Outcome, and Obsessions for each role.

Think about the first half of the first day a new employee has on the job as their onboarding to the organization. This should be designed as a process for all new employees to get them set up for all of their benefits and payroll, introduced to the company history (if that wasn't covered in the interview process), the vision, and so on. The second half of the day can then be used for them to spend with the person to whom they report, getting them introduced to their team, going over the accountabilities based on the Next Level Accountability Chart, and introducing them to the system they will be using for their training. This should include going over where the Process Playbooks are housed, how they can access them, and which sections apply to their role and need to be studied. The leader should have an outline of what their first week will look like, including what training should be completed and who they will be working with or shadowing.

At the end of the first week, we recommend a meeting, just fifteen to thirty minutes, that is designed to be conversational and start with core values. The leader does a quick check-in with the employee with a few open-ended questions like, "How are you feeling after your first week?" or "How are things going for you compared to how you expected them to go?" Just something to get them talking and engaged. Then, you can start talking through the core values.

For example, at Next Level Growth, the first of our four core values is "Take Ownership." If I'm the one onboarding a new team member, I'll start by saying something like, "So, as you know, our first core value here is to take ownership. Now that you've been here for a week, I'd love to get your thoughts on how you're feeling about that core value. Is what we expect clear? Do you feel like we're authentic about it as an organization? Is there anything you don't understand or want to ask about?"

The point is to have a brief conversation about the value, to make sure that the new employee is getting their questions answered, and also to help them begin to see that, as their leader, you want their feedback on how they feel the organization is doing. You want them to understand that you desire a culture where it is okay for team members to come to their leaders with concerns. When it feels like time to move on, simply move on to the next core value and repeat this process until you're done with the core values.

After finishing the conversation about core values, move right into their Mission, Most Critical Outcome, and Obsessions—their MMOs. Similar to the conversation around core values, go over their Mission together. Make sure they understand the specific words, talk about what expectations look like, and ask them how they are feeling about their mission and their ability to achieve it. As their leader, share your early observations after week one and ask questions to get them talking about how they see things from their perspective.

Do the same thing for their Most Critical Outcome, their MCO, and make sure they understand what is being measured, how it is being calculated, and where they can find the data. Make sure they understand what the key drivers are that help them achieve their MCO and that they are focusing on those drivers.

Finally, talk through each of their Obsessions with them in the same manner. Ask for their input on how things are working for them, give them your feedback around what you're observing, and make sure they are getting their questions answered.

For example, if you are a leadership team member onboarding a new manager and their first obsession is to "Lead, manage, retain and hold my team accountable," you could ask them open-ended questions to start a conversation like: How are you feeling about your team? Have you been able to get some one-on-one time to get to know them and start building relationships with them? Are they doing a good job of staying on task, and are you clear on how to support and manage them? Is there anyone struggling with accountability, and do you have a handle on how to work with them to make improvements?

If another of their obsessions is to "Follow the Sales Playbook," then consider questions like: Have you been through our Sales Playbook? Do you have any questions or concerns that will prevent you from following it and properly executing the steps? Do you feel comfortable that our Playbook will get the outcomes we are seeking? Is there anything you are seeing in the Playbook that you think we can make better or more effective?

Having some specific but open-ended questions to start a conversation with your direct reports will go a long way in establishing clear expectations and helping you, as their leader, identify areas where you can be most supportive and effective in setting them up to be successful quickly.

When you're done talking through the core values and their MMOs, consider ending with three simple questions that can go a long way toward building a strong relationship with new team members.

1. Is there anything you need from me that you aren't getting? Resources, time, training, clear expectations?
2. Is there anything going on that is frustrating you or making it difficult to work here?
3. Is there anything I'm doing that is making it difficult to work for me?

These three questions, especially the last one, will begin to help the new team members see that you genuinely have their back and are here to support them. It will help them see that you are also an empathetic and self-aware leader. This equates to someone they can trust. While they may be reluctant to open up too much the first time you do this, if you use the cadence we suggest, you will find that by the end of their first ninety days, they will be much more open and honest with you, and that helps you tremendously as a leader.

This process also prepares the new team member for Quarterly Calibrations, which we will discuss in the next chapter, "A Culture of Performance." Quarterly Calibrations are used to develop and retain A-Players and keep them at their best throughout their careers.

When it comes to frequency, keeping in mind that the meeting described above was at the end of their first week on the job, we recommend doing this again at the end of their second week on the job, at their one-month anniversary, the forty-five-day mark, their second month anniversary, and the end of their first ninety days. This means that each new team member will have this kind of meeting, a step back from the day-to-day and a high-level look at their role, six times in their first ninety days. If their leader is disciplined enough to stay focused and keep these meetings to thirty minutes or less, it will take them no more than three hours over three months for each new team member. When you think of all the benefits of a well-onboarded new team member, the Return on Investment for the small amount of time it takes is massive.

To successfully manage time through meetings like this, consider a few of the following best practices:

- Schedule the meeting to have a hard stop at thirty minutes and communicate that in the beginning.
- Consider having a thirty-minute timer visible. When time is being measured, especially with a countdown timer, people tend to stay more focused and on topic.
- Whenever it feels like the conversation is going off on

a tangent, be quick and intentional about stopping and bringing the conversation back to the point at hand.

- Stay focused on identifying issues with your new hire and discussing solutions.
- Avoid storytelling and stick to the point.

Based on feedback from hundreds of clients following this approach, by the end of the first ninety days, one of three things happens:

1. The leader realizes they made a bad hire and exits the person during their probationary period.
2. The new employee realizes there is nowhere to hide from accountability in the organization, and they quit within their first ninety days.
3. The leader confirms they made a good hire who is on track after their first ninety days, and the new team member feels that they have built a positive, open relationship with their leader and they are well equipped for success in their role.

The latter of those three things is by far the most common outcome, and the companies who do this consistently have the lowest turnover and the highest employee satisfaction scores of all the companies we work with.

PROCESS PLAYBOOKS— DO IT YOURSELF

When thinking about Playbooks as high-level checklists, think about the Pareto Principle, also known as the 80/20 Rule, that 80 percent of your results come from 20 percent of your inputs, so document the 20 percent that gets you the 80 percent. Where more detail would be helpful, as I outlined earlier, we suggest creating a video library to supplement the Process Playbooks. Many people are used to learning from content like YouTube videos, so consider creating screen share videos for detailed instructions on how to do things within your CRM, ERP, or HRIS systems as part of the training for employees.

You can even use simple cell phone videos to show employees how to complete steps of your Process Playbooks that will provide them with greater detail. Some of our manufacturing clients use cell phone videos to show the details of how to set up a machine and other technical aspects of production. We have hospitality clients who use simple videos to provide training details on how to greet a guest and how to address and work with an unhappy guest. If a picture is worth a thousand words, a video is worth many more.

A word of caution about taking the do-it-yourself approach to documenting your processes. You will likely focus more on documenting what you already do than you will on process optimization as you go. If you don't outsource the work, as explained in the next section, you should seriously consider working with my clone at **AskMichaelErath.com** for help along the way.

The following approach is a simple way to begin documenting your processes and building out your playbooks on your own. Unless you are a small organization, this will be a heavy lift, but something you should be able to complete, along with everything else you're working on, within about a nine- to twelve-month time frame. For most organizations, we recommend outsourcing the heavy lifting to experts. More on that shortly. First, here's a process to do it yourself.

Step 1

Make an initial list of the Process Playbooks you want to create. Common playbooks include People Journey, Marketing, Sales (or Business Development), Operations, Accounting, IT, and Client Satisfaction/Customer Service. Many organizations choose to start with the area where they have the greatest pain points, realizing that if they start there, they eliminate the biggest sources of pain and frustration first. It is common to end up with somewhere between ten and twenty critical playbooks, and it takes most organizations close to a year to get everything done when taking the do-it-yourself approach.

Step 2

Determine who needs to participate in creating each of your playbooks. It is always best to include a handful of your best employees for each segment of the business you will be systemizing through your playbooks. You want to build your playbooks around your best people. Set aside two hours per team to get started and bring everyone together in a meeting room. We recommend using 4 x 6 Post-it notes for the process and using different colors for different components of the process, which can be helpful and will be described below.

> Note: The following examples will be for a hypothetical Sales Playbook.

Step 3

The team leader starts by asking the following questions, getting alignment from the team around each, and writing the agreed-upon answer on a Post-it note, one per question. The leader then puts the Post-its on the far-left side of one wall, each one below the note before it.

The questions are:

1. **What is the overall purpose of this playbook?** (Ex: "To qualify leads and convert them to a signed contract")
2. **What happens to trigger this process to start?** That is your input. (Ex: "New lead identified")
3. **What is the playbook's desired outcome?** (Ex: "Contract properly completed, signed, and delivered to operations team for scheduling")
4. **What should we measure around this playbook?** (Ex: "Number of leads to goal, Speed of initial response to goal, Dollar value of opportunities, Conversion rate")
5. **Who receives the handoff from this playbook?** (Ex: "Scheduling Team Leader")
6. **Who owns this playbook?** (Ex: "Sales Manager")

Step 4

The team leader asks the team, "What is the trigger that starts our process?" In this case, a lead is identified. When it comes to leads, it is common to get leads through multiple sources, like referrals, web sign-ups, outbound marketing, and more. Once you've identified the trigger, then ask, "What is the very first thing we should be doing?" The focus is not on what you do, but what you *should* do—always use this process to improve the way you do things as you begin to document it. If you should be doing things differently for a first step with a referral than you would a web sign-up, make sure you clarify that in the process.

Once you have the right answer, put this first step on a different color Post-it note. (Ex: "Enter all available lead contact information into our CRM")

Next, ask, "Are there any sub-steps we need to capture?" If so, put the sub-steps below the primary steps on the wall. (Ex: "Add notes and attach documents as necessary.")

Conclude by asking, "Is that it for this step, and is there anything that needs to be improved or further clarified here?" Also, be sure to ask, "Are there any issues or frustrations with this step that we need to address?"

If there are no issues or frustrations, move on. If there are, you can either solve it with the team and write it into the process, or if you cannot solve it quickly as a team, then identify it as an issue and capture it below the playbook step on a different color Post-it note for future issues to resolve.

Step 5

The team leader starts by asking, "What is the very next thing that should happen?" Then, follow up with questions to optimize the playbook:

1. Are there any sub-steps we need to capture?
2. Is that it for this step, and is there anything that needs to be improved or further clarified here?
3. Are there any issues or frustrations with this step that we need to address?

Continue repeating Step 5 until you reach the end of the process and document the actual handoff. Take photos of the Post-it notes, or number them in sequence (use numbers for the main steps and the same number with letters for each sub-step) and use that to build your playbook document or add to your LMS. Confirm that you have all the right measurables, and make sure they are added to the team's Scorecard so you can track the activities and ensure the playbook is being properly used and getting you the results you intended.

Once your processes are documented and organized, you need to distribute them to everyone and work through them with every employee so that, for their role, regardless of tenure, all employees are clear on the processes they are expected to follow. This also allows you to clarify what you need them to do when they encounter nuances, or situations that are nonstandard and require deviation from the process. How much room do they have to figure out a solution on their own? How much input do they need to get from management?

That last part is summarized beautifully by Isadore Sharp, founder of the Four Seasons, who believed that you systemize the predictable so you can humanize the exceptional.

The more we can systemize the predictable things that happen within our organizations, the more we free people to use their creative minds to humanize everything else and create exceptional experiences both inside and outside the organization.

Download a sample Process Playbook for The Employee Journey, and other forms and examples, at FiveObsessions.com.

A FASTER AND BETTER
PATH TO DONE

In our experience, it takes most organizations who go down the do-it-yourself path of documenting their Process Playbooks anywhere from nine months to nine years to get the work done. The problem is that they often overcomplicate it, or ironically, they get too busy in the day-to-day firefighting that would be significantly reduced if they had their Process Playbooks in place.

At Next Level Growth, we often introduce and refer our clients to experts in the field of process documentation who can come in and do the heavy lifting for them, often working with teams to deliver their Process Playbooks in just a matter of weeks. Many of these experts will come to our clients' locations and work with teams and key stakeholders around each process to extract the actual process following an approach similar to what I have described above. When that is done, they do the work of creating the documentation and then submitting it back to our clients as an over-80-percent-done working draft of their first Process Playbooks.

If you would like an introduction to one of our preferred partners, just visit NextLevelGrowth.com and click on "Start a Conversation." Make sure to include in the message field that you're looking for a Process Playbook connection.

OPTIMIZING YOUR PROCESSES

Once your processes are documented and you have your Process Playbooks in place, including strong onboarding and recurring training systems, it is critical to ensure that your playbooks stay current and optimized. There are two primary ways to do this.

Organic Optimization

A great way to make sure you are organically optimizing your processes is actually built into how we like to teach our clients to tackle their issues. As you go through the day-to-day of your business, whenever issues arise, whether sales issues, operational issues, accounting issues, or anything else, always address the issue by asking, "Do we have a defined and documented process that should have prevented this situation?" If the answer is no, you need to establish and implement a process. Likely, once you have your Process Playbooks in place, the answer will be that you do have a process for that situation, but the process either needs another step or needs a step to be improved.

For example, one of our clients is an HVAC distributor who sells equipment and parts to HVAC contractors. Their Process Playbooks had been in place for years, and they were having an issue between the operations team and the sales team that their Next Level Growth Business Guide was able to smoke out in one of their meetings. When a customer would have a problem with new equipment they were installing, there was a process in place for their customer to submit what they call a TSA Request. A TSA is a technical service advisor and is a person who would help the contractor in the field troubleshoot their issue. TSAs are part of the operations team.

When a TSA Request was received, the TSA would review it and work with the contractor to reach a solution. Occasionally, the contractor would not accept the proposed solution, and depending on how the TSA handled the objection, the relationship with the contractor could be damaged. When this happened, it had a negative impact on the salesperson who was responsible for maintaining the contractor relationship and growing their business. This could eventually impact the salesperson's compensation and was causing occasional stress between the sales and operations teams. When their Business Guide asked them if they had a process in place that should prevent that issue, the initial answer was "yes." But their Guide asked them to explain the process as he mapped it out on the whiteboard, and in doing so, they identified the missing step that was occasionally causing the friction between the two teams (see image).

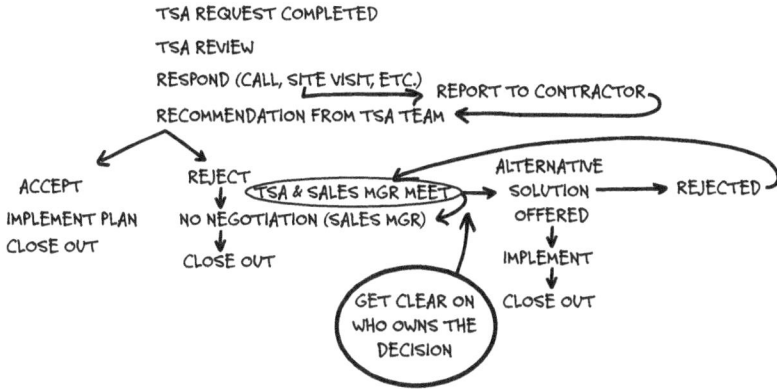

Figure 5.2

The first few steps were very straightforward.

1. The first step is that a TSA request would be submitted by the customer. That would be the triggering event that would put this playbook in motion.
2. The TSA Request would immediately go to a TSA for review.
3. After review, the TSA would respond to the contractor, either by phone call or site visit, depending on the nature of the issue.
4. Following the response, which could require more than one communication or site visit, the TSA would make a recommendation to the contractor. The recommendation could be something like:
   a. The TSA explaining to the contractor how to resolve the problem in the field
   b. The TSA authorizing that a defective or damaged part be replaced
   c. The TSA replacing the entire system the contractor had purchased

5. At this point, there were two possible outcomes. The contractor would either accept the solution, in which case the TSA would jump to the final two steps, implement the solution, and close out the TSA request, or the contractor would reject the solution, and the process would continue as follows (*in rare occasions, if the contractor was being unreasonable, the TSA had the authority not to offer any further solutions or negotiations, and simply move to closing out the request, but that was not common*).

6. If the solution was not acceptable to the contractor, this next step would involve offering an alternative solution, which, if accepted, would lead to implementation and TSA request closeout. If the alternative solution was not accepted, they would remain in this stage of offering alternative solutions and negotiation until either something was accepted or the TSA decided to stop the process and close out the ticket without a resolution.

It was in Step 6 where sometimes the TSA would decide to simply replace the entire system, which could easily be a ten-thousand-dollar decision, or they could decide to end the process and not agree to a solution, which would leave the contractor upset. The missing link was that the salesperson, who was responsible for maintaining the contractor relationship and growing their business, did not have a voice in this process that potentially had an impact on the relationship that they had built with the contractor and were responsible to maintain and grow. Not only that, but this was normally happening without them knowing that the contractor was even having a problem in the field.

As their Guide worked with them to find a solution, he pressed them to really dig into how they could improve Step 6 in a way that would resolve this issue. It quickly became clear to both the vice president of sales and the vice president of operations that if the initial solution offered in Step 4 was rejected, and any obvious alternative solutions were also rejected, it would be normal for the contractor to begin getting frustrated. At this stage, the TSA and contractor would often begin a negotiation process to try to reach a solution, and it was decided in the meeting that before any further solutions were offered or negotiations were had to try to reach a resolution, the TSA would escalate the ticket and bring in a manager from the sales team to review the situation and get involved in negotiating a resolution.

One other item the team needed to get clear on was in this updated negotiation process where both the TSA and the sales manager were collaborating to reach a positive outcome with the contractor. Who actually needed to own and be accountable for the final decision? Because this company was very clear that part of its purpose and differentiation strategy was making the customer experience of primary importance, they agreed the final decision should rest with sales. If, on the other hand, the company had been focused on short-term shareholder value and maximizing profits, they would likely have left the decision with the TSA. This is an example of how being clear on your purpose helps you define processes that are in alignment with what matters most to your organization.

In working to resolve an issue between two teams, they discovered a weakness in one of their processes, worked together to review the process to find out where a step could be made better, and then modified and optimized their process. By doing so, they eliminated the internal friction between their teams, which allowed the sales team, which owns the relationship with the contractor, to make the final decision. They also reduced the number of times a contractor had a bad experience because they could not reach a favorable solution with someone who was wired by nature to be technical and not necessarily a relationship builder.

AUDITING FOR OPTIMIZATION

While the process above will help optimize your playbooks as issues arise, it will not ensure that all of your Process Playbooks remain optimized. To prevent your playbooks from becoming outdated, you need a simple and consistent process in place to audit and review your playbooks.

If you think about the Next Level Accountability Chart and Obsessions, as we discussed in Chapter 4, each member of an executive team should have an obsession to own their team's playbooks, execution, and outcomes. For example, a vice president of sales might have a Sales Playbook with sections like:

- Onboarding a New Prospect
- The First Communications and Establishing Trust
- The Discovery Process
- Matching a Solution to the Prospect's Needs
- Overcoming Objections
- Closing the Sale
- Contracting
- The Handoff to Operations

Because one part of the VP of sales' obsession around "owning" the playbook includes owning its currency and relevancy, we like to teach that at least once per year, the leadership team member who owns the process should get together with a handful of their key team members, the ones who are really the best of their best and do a review of all of their team's Process Playbooks. In doing so, they want to challenge the processes to see, since the last review, if any of them have come up with a better way to do something or encountered a problem as a result of something in the playbook that needs to be improved. By taking a creative approach to reimagining their process, they often will come up with new ideas to make them even better.

Another step that can help keep your Process Playbooks optimal is to have a few of the key stakeholders on the team that your own team hands things off to review *your* playbooks to see if you are doing something in your processes that unknowingly causes problems or inefficiencies for their team. In the example above, the VP of sales might ask the VP of operations to review the Contracting and Hand-off to Operations sections of the Sales Playbook with key operations team stakeholders to provide feedback from a different perspective.

A recent example of this came up when I was checking in with one of my clients and the director of operations mentioned that they had done a review of the sales team's process for writing up an order. In doing so, they realized that one of the challenges they were having in operations could easily be resolved if the sales team obtained one additional piece of information and added a new field on the sales order to capture that information. Simply adding that one item would allow the operations team to know something that had been missing before they started working on the customer's order and would eliminate the issue they were having. They had explained this to their sales director, who immediately implemented and communicated the change, and the problem went away.

If every leadership team member does this just once per year, the Process Playbooks will remain current and optimized and deliver extraordinary results for your organization.

Remember, almost all of your issues can be traced back to either a people issue or a process issue, and without *Optimized Playbooks*, you may have people with the potential to be great who simply don't have the necessary clarity to know the right way to do their jobs and are actually being penalized, or exited, because you failed to give them a key resource to be successful. Only once you have your systems designed and aligned to create excellent outcomes through *Optimized Playbooks* with effective training (practice) and coaching in place can you truly create an accountable *Culture of Performance*, the fourth of the Five Obsession of Elite Organizations.

Chapter 6

OBSESSION #4: A CULTURE OF PERFORMANCE

"Things in life don't pay off on
effort, but on results."

—HARVEY MACKAY

Legendary college basketball coach John Wooden famously said we should "Never mistake activity for achievement."[23] While it takes the right activities, done the right way, and the right number of times to achieve success, in my years as an entrepreneur and now Business Guide, I have seen firsthand that far too many organizations give teams and leaders a pass for too long because they are doing the activities, even when they are not achieving the desired results.

---

23 John Wooden and Steve Jamison, *Wooden: A Lifetime of Observations and Reflections On and Off the Court* (McGraw-Hill, 1997), 8.

Building a high-performing culture into an organization is hard work and takes time. It requires a special discipline, focus, and drive to do things at a high level and to a high standard all of the time. It is also highly dependent on getting the first three of the Five Obsessions right.

First and foremost, you must have *Great People*, which is why it is the first of the Five Obsessions. You need people who share your core values and whose natural behaviors are highly aligned with those values. And you need people who not only have the experience and skills but also the drive to perform in their specific roles to a high standard every day.

Those *Great People* need to be provided with an *Inspiring Purpose*, one that they can embrace at a deep emotional level and make their own. They need to understand how success in their role contributes to a bigger picture, how what they do affects other teams, the customer or client, and ultimately, the organization and where it is trying to go in the marketplace or in the world.

In the earlier chapter on *Inspiring Purpose*, I discussed the importance of defining and driving the right strategy to differentiate yourself and provide consistent value in the marketplace. With the addition of a Just Cause and Daily Purpose, people can get clear on why you are in the game that you are in, and they can decide if they want to be a part of it. Adding in a clearly defined Summit helps them understand where this journey will take the organization, and then they can decide if successfully reaching that Summit will be worth the effort it will take. Some will be up for the challenge, and others will not. You want to build on the former and let the latter go on to other organizations. They will not help you drive your organization to its Summit because they don't have the emotional connection, passion, and drive to remain disciplined and focused on the journey.

Those inspired, *Great People* need their leaders to provide them with the systems, processes, and playbooks to consistently and seamlessly operate in an optimal way that creates both internal and external raving fans. This leads to a systemized business where work flows clearly and efficiently through the teams and the organization.

You must get these first three obsessions right to even have a chance at building a successful *Culture of Performance.*

KEYS TO A CULTURE OF PERFORMANCE

There are five foundational components to building a *Culture of Performance*. While in total, there are certainly more things you can focus on to enhance performance, at a foundational level, if you will first focus on getting these five things right, you will have the building blocks you need to create a consistently high-performing organization. They are:

- Scorecards and Scoreboards
- Growth Rocks
- The Right Meeting Rhythms
- A Feedback Loop
- A Coaching System

SCORECARDS AND SCOREBOARDS— THE DIFFERENCE

Imagine watching two teams playing basketball, but nobody is keeping score, there is no clock measuring the time remaining, and there are no coaches keeping other data points or statistics. It would be like watching practice and probably would not be very interesting. I would also expect that the level of effort being put forth by the players would be less than their absolute best.

Compare that, however, to the way teams perform when there is a scoreboard. We know the score, the time remaining, what the team foul situation is, and how many time-outs are left. The coaches keep up with the statistics, report back to the team during time-outs with what the data is telling them, and make adjustments accordingly. Suddenly, when we're keeping score, the effort and focus improves, and the game is more exciting.

Scorecards

Similarly, at Next Level Growth, we define scorecards as the data sets that teams look at in their Weekly Tactical Meetings to review the week's performance, evaluate what the numbers are telling them, make adjustments, and set action items accordingly. The data on scorecards lets the team know where they are performing to expectations and where they are coming up short.

In Chapter 3, we discussed Most Critical Outcome (MCO), the single most critical and measurable outcomes-based number that a person must meet to be successful in their role. Each MCO typically has two to four key drivers. Of the many things that you could measure, these are the two to four that are the most impactful leading activities that drive the MCO. These are the items that go on a team's weekly scorecard.

At a leadership team level, if you have a founder, a vice president of business development, a vice president of operations, and a vice president of finance, they each have one MCO, so the team has a total of four MCOs. This means that their leadership team scorecard should have somewhere between eight and sixteen numbers that they track and report on every week in their Weekly Tactical Meeting.

Scoreboards

A scoreboard, on the other hand, is just like a scoreboard in any sport. It is the performance information that needs to be visible to the players on the field so they can always have a reference to know how they are performing while they are playing the game.

Scorecards, Scoreboards, and Performance: A Personal Example

It is a psychological fact that people perform differently when they know how they are performing against certain goals or against other individuals or teams. I recently took up cycling as a form of exercise. Since I'm purely doing this for the exercise, I passed on getting an expensive road bike and settled for a hybrid city bike. I've got a ten-mile route I ride several days per week, and there is about five hundred feet of elevation change. As a novice looking for exercise, it's a good route. When I started riding, it was taking me about forty-five minutes to complete the circuit.

I use an app to track my time, distance, average speed, and a few other points of data. I keep the app mounted to the bike and am able to see, in real time, things like elapsed time, current speed, average speed, and distance. This is my "scoreboard." One particular day, as I was climbing a 1.5-mile hill on the route, another cyclist passed me. Granted, he had a nice road bike and all the fancy gear and cycling clothes while I was in gym shorts, a T-shirt, and sneakers…but I was still frustrated at the thought of being passed. In response, I put forth more effort, changed gears to pick up a little more speed, and was actually able to stay on pace with him for the rest of the climb.

What I realized was no different than what we observe with the teams we coach. When challenged, our naturally competitive spirit will drive most of us to level up our performance. I also realized that when I was competing against only myself and my own stats, I was allowing myself to settle into something less than my best effort. I only woke up when someone passed me by. I found another gear. Now I know that I can push harder and go faster. Now I ride against the last version of myself. I was also able to reference my scoreboard to see, when keeping up with the other rider climbing that hill, what my new speed was. Climbing this hill, I'm normally in a gear and putting forth an effort that keeps me between 7 and 7.5 miles per hour. While keeping up with the other cyclist, I noticed that I was staying between 8.5 and 9 miles per hour, so now I have a new expectation of myself when climbing that same hill.

When I finish a ride, I put stats on a whiteboard in my office, my score-card, and I track them week by week. Since I keep the same route, I just track the time I started the ride and the time it took me to complete the ride. Every time I ride, I try to beat the guy I was the last time I rode. As a result, just a few weeks later, I broke the forty-minute mark twice. The prior version of me, the one that took forty-five minutes to complete the circuit, would have been 1.1 miles behind me when I finished. That's an 11 percent improvement in my performance, and I'm just a hack cyclist doing this for exercise.

Scoreboards and Performance: An Example from the Field

The same strategy can apply to growing your profits. When I was president and CEO of Erath Veneer, we had four production lines, each running on two shifts, slicing hardwood veneer for the furniture, door, and panel industries. In all, we had eight different production teams.

We worked hard on and gained clarity around our Profit per X, a concept from *Good to Great* that I will further explain in Chapter 8. In our case, it was *Dollars of Gross Profit per Board Foot Produced*. We realized that of the many areas in which we could make adjustments and implement strategies to improve the ratio that drove our economic engine, focusing on and consistently improving our throughput in terms of board feet would be one area that would make us more efficient and more profitable.

We started by analyzing historical data on throughput and supplemented that by running tests and time studies. This analysis allowed us to determine, by specie produced (think of species for us like a "product line"), how much throughput per hour each production team should average for an eight-hour shift depending on the mix of species they were producing during a particular shift and depending on which production line was being used.

To make sure we didn't sacrifice quality for the sake of efficiency, we added limit switches to each veneer slicer that would turn on a light at the same part of every log being sliced, and that would cue the team to pull a sample, which they would then label with the production line number, shift, time, and log number. The following morning, our production manager and sales manager would review the samples together and reject anything that did not meet our standards. Requiring the two positions to collaborate in the review prevented a situation where operations would be policing itself and possibly covering up mistakes. For any mis-manufactured samples, the team that produced the damaged product would have the board footage of that log deducted from their prior day's totals. This removed any incentive to sacrifice quality for speed and volume.

After the samples were reviewed, our office staff would tally each of the eight production teams' results from the prior day, and we would print a color bar graph that showed a thick black line where each team's goal was for the prior day, along with a vertical bar indicating their actual results. If they fell short of their goal, the bar was red. If they met or exceeded their goal, the bar was green. We kept a rolling week of graphs up on the wall by the door to the break room so every employee in the company saw the results. Nobody wanted to be on the teams that were consistently in the red.

Without any financial incentives, and just by displaying the data and letting everyone see how their team was doing relative to the other teams, we saw an 8 percent increase in average throughput per shift. That improvement in productivity, with a balanced focus on quality, lowered our unit cost, which increased our Profit per X—our Dollars of Gross Profit per Board Foot Produced.

Once we had consistent data to prove that we were doing the right things on our production lines and tracking the data properly, we reinvested some of the financial gains into a bonus program for the production teams that created a true meritocracy on the plant floor, increasing total compensation for the best-performing teams. As a result of the clarity, visibility, and focus on results, team members would go out of their way to help each other as needed to keep their productivity up, and team leads would be quick to communicate with their supervisors when an underperformer was holding them back and needed more training or, in some cases, to be exited from the team.

As an organization, it is critical to make sure that you are tracking and providing sufficient visibility to the right data to drive the performance you want and using that data to create a healthy spirit of competition… something for which A-Players hunger.

GROWTH ROCKS

In his 1994 book *First Things First*, Stephen Covey introduced a concept he called "Rocks." In Covey's metaphor, Rocks represent the most important priorities in life or work that should be scheduled and addressed first, before less important activities which he represented as pebbles. On our Next Level Growth YouTube channel, there is a playlist we call "Client Favorites." It is a playlist of the most requested videos among the ones we often share with our clients to help set context or support the messaging around something we're working through.

On that list is a video called "Big Rocks." The video features Stephen Covey demonstrating the Rocks metaphor. In it, he asks a woman from the audience to come up on stage. He has two large clear plastic containers on a table which he says represent the finite amount of time we have, our capacity. He also has several rocks, each about the size of a baseball, and a container filled with pebbles.

He explains to the woman from the audience that the rocks represent the big, important things in her life, both personal and professional. The pebbles, he says, are all the small things, including all the noise and distractions we have in our lives.

He starts by explaining that what most people do is begin their days by allowing themselves to get pulled into all the noise and distractions, which are the small things. As he is saying this, he takes the container of small pebbles and pours them into the empty container, representing her capacity. Then he asks her to put the rocks in, the big, important things. One at a time, she does, but she cannot get them all to fit. He reinforces his point that when we let ourselves get distracted by all the noise, we often don't have time for the important things.

Then, he asks her to reverse the order. To take the big rocks and put them in the other empty container, but to put them in first. When she is done, he asks her to then pour all the small pebbles from the first container into the new one. As she does, the small pebbles begin to fill in the open spaces between the rocks, making their way to the bottom of the container. As she continues, eventually all of the pebbles fit into the container…the same size container that everything would not fit into when the order was reversed.

We like to use the "Rock" metaphor when we talk about the big, important growth projects that people need to take on. These are things that help organizations and people grow, and unfortunately, they are often the things that get deprioritized on a daily basis because we get far too distracted either putting out fires or dealing with small things. Rocks are also things that are not going to get done in the normal day-to-day course of business unless they are called out, a specific timeline is established, and a single person takes on accountability to ensure they get done properly and on time.

Examples of Growth Rocks

One important thing to be sure of when you set a Rock is that you are absolutely clear on two things. First, what is it, specifically, that you are looking to accomplish? Second, how will you know it is successfully done?

Far too many times we see companies who come to us after using other business operating systems that also use the popular Rocks concept that have struggled to achieve results because their Rocks are poorly written. When we onboard a new leadership team through our Base Camp process, we teach and help them create their Next Level Accountability Chart for the leadership team seats on the very first day. Our third and final day of Base Camp is usually two to three months later and is the point in time when we expect them to have their Next Level Accountability Chart complete and finalized for the entire organization.

As that is a project that is not part of their normal day-to-day responsibilities, we treat it as a Growth Rock (from this point forward, I will use the terms Rock and Growth Rock interchangeably). In order to answer the two questions posed above, we encourage each team member to take on a Rock that will be due on the last day of Base Camp. Base Camp is the first phase of our engagement with a client and is a time when we work through all of the foundational components of our approach with the leadership team. In this case, the Rock is usually written as:

> The Next Level Accountability Chart, with a clear Mission, Most Critical Outcome, and Obsessions®, is documented for every position in my reporting structure and agreed to by the leadership team.

The way this Rock is written makes it clear what they are looking to accomplish, and they will know it is successfully done when it has been agreed to by the leadership team.

Milestones

It's one thing to have a well-written Rock with a clear due date, and it is something else entirely to successfully complete the Rock on time. It is human nature to procrastinate, and we consistently find that when organizations do not use milestones for their Rocks, people tend to put off getting started. As a result, like a student cramming for final exams the night before, they do a rushed job and either complete the Rock but do it poorly, or they end up missing the deadline and needing to push it further into the future.

To overcome this, we encourage our clients to set milestones. Milestones are the smaller, time-bound steps that must get done on time to keep the overall Rock on track. Sticking with our Rock around completing the Next Level Accountability Chart, a series of milestones might look like:

- Evaluate and document the ideal structure for my team and compare it to our current structure to determine if any changes need to be made
- For each of my direct reports, draft what I believe to be their Mission, Most Critical Outcome, and two to six obsessions
- Meet with each of my direct reports to discuss and review the draft of their seat and make any adjustments necessary based on our conversations
- Collaborate with each of my direct reports to build out all of the seats that report up to their role
- Present my function's Next Level Accountability Chart to the leadership team for feedback and approval

By clarifying those five major steps, the leader can then begin to set dates. If the Rock is due in ten weeks, they might set a due date for their first milestone to be due at the end of week one and the second milestone to be due at the end of week two. Perhaps they give themselves until the end of week four to complete the third milestone and then until week seven to complete the fourth. The fifth and final milestone might be something they want to complete by the end of week eight so that if there is feedback from the leadership team that requires adjustments to be made, they still have two weeks to get that done. Otherwise, they completed their Rock early, which is never a bad thing.

Here is a form that we encourage our clients to use to help them plan out their Rocks and Milestones. I've filled out the form with an example of a Rock for a new sales manager to build out ramp plans for newly onboarded salespeople. This might be something that is taken on as a Rock if an issue arises around inconsistency that ends up being the result of an organization not having clear ramp plans for new team members.

Note: You can download a PDF of this form at FiveObsessions.com.

| Name: | Jim Halpert | | Due Date: | September 30 |

Use the contents of the box below to create the wording of the Rock you enter in the software.

What do you want to accomplish in one clear sentence and **how will you know it is successfully done?**

Six month ramp plan for new Dunder Mifflin sales team members defined, documented, and rolled out with clear measurables, tracking, and coaching process in place to ensure all new sales team members are consistently at or above goal by the end of their first six months.

Milestones: What must get done to achieve the Rock?

		WHO	START IN	BY WHEN
Milestone	Draft outcomes expectations by month for each of the first 6 months for a new sales team member and send to Phyllis and Stanley for feedback.	Jim	ASAP	July 20
Milestone	Review draft of ramp expectations, add comments as necessary, and return to Jim.	Phyllis and Stanley	July 20	July 31
Milestone	Update draft ramp plan based on feedback.	Jim	July 31	August 10
Milestone	Define and document process to measure and track activities and outcomes by person relative to ramp plan.	Jim	August 10	August 17
Milestone	Define and document coaching process and meeting structure for new employees to receive supportive coaching throughout their ramp.	Jim	August 17	August 24
Milestone	Present ramp plan, metrics, and coaching process to Michael for revisions and ultimately final approval.	Jim	August 24	September 15
Milestone	Implement new ramp plan, metrics, and coaching process with Sales Team, including all necessary training.	Jim	September 15	September 30

NextLevelGrowth.com

© 2025 Next Level Growth

Figure 6.1

Download this form and more at FiveObsessions.com

When we break big projects down into smaller pieces, or milestones, they often feel less overwhelming and much more manageable.

THE RIGHT MEETING RHYTHMS

Let me start by saying that nobody should be in meetings that are not highly valuable and a very good use of their time. In his book, *Meetings Suck*, my friend and author Cameron Herold makes the case that meetings themselves are not inherently bad or a waste of time; rather, it's poorly organized and run meetings that are the problem. He argues that when meetings are conducted effectively—with a clear purpose, proper planning, and engaged participants—they can be one of the most valuable tools for driving business success.

Weekly Tactical Meeting

At Next Level Growth, we teach what we refer to as a Weekly Tactical Meeting. This meeting is intended for leadership teams, and often the top level of departmental teams, and is our evolution and improvement on meeting agendas we've seen in and used from Scaling Up, EOS, and our own experiences. Typically, beyond the departmental team, as you get closer to the front lines, we recommend Daily Huddles, which I will cover in the next section of this chapter.

The Weekly Tactical Meeting was named to be very clear. It is a weekly meeting that is intended to keep tactical execution on point, keep the team performing at a high level, and ensure you are quickly addressing anywhere that there is a breakdown or a problem. I have learned over my career that every meeting should have clear objectives and a clear agenda to achieve those objectives. At Next Level Growth, we encourage our clients to refuse to attend any meeting that does not have clearly defined and communicated objectives and an agenda to achieve those objectives. As Cameron Herold likes to say, *"No agenda, no attenda."* [24]

One more thought on your meetings. Somebody needs to be in charge of running the meeting and keeping the team focused and on task. We like to suggest that the best person for running your meetings is the best person at managing time and politely cutting other people off. If your meeting facilitator cannot interrupt and challenge team members when he or she feels like people are getting off track or talking in circles, your meetings will not be as effective as you want them to be.

Objectives: There are three objectives of the Weekly Tactical Meeting:

- Stay aligned and connected as a team
- Keep the numbers and priorities on track
- Identify and resolve the key issues

That's it. Anything that is not directly contributing to one of those three objectives should not be part of the meeting but rather addressed offline. Time is money, and when you consider the fully burdened cost of everyone sitting in the meeting, plus the opportunity cost of them not being out in the organization doing what they do, a sixty- or ninety-minute meeting is not cheap, so it needs to be treated accordingly.

While we highly encourage our clients to customize their meetings to work best for them, we offer the following agenda as a starting point and find that this works very well for the majority of them. At a leadership team level, we ask that they start by blocking ninety minutes once per week. Over time, as teams get better at running these

---

24 Cameron Herold, *Double Double: How to Double Your Revenue and Profit in 3 Years or Less* (Greenleaf Book Group Press, 2011).

meetings, they typically finish early, but it is always helpful to have the time blocked off for when you need it.

Agenda

Check-In *(Five Minutes)*

The meeting starts with a quick, five-minute Check-In. The intention is to create a buffer between whatever noise and distractions each attendee has been facing that day and the meeting space, where they need to be able to take a step back from the noise of the day-to-day. We encourage them to think of the business like a snow globe. For just ninety minutes every week, they are going to step out of that snow globe and look at things from the outside in. When you're too close to the issues, it is often difficult to think about them in a clear and objective way, and we find this analogy to be helpful in getting teams into the right mindset to effectively solve issues.

So that things don't become stale over time, the questions for the Check-In can be modified, but they should be intentional. When we start working with a team, they often don't know that much about each other outside of work, and we want to see some of those walls come down. Getting to know each other on a more human level helps to build trust. The more teams connect and grow closer and more trusting, the easier it is for them to deal with the difficult things and have the hard conversations they need to have if they are truly going to build something elite.

Consider using the following three Check-In questions to get people talking and connecting:

1. *What is something positive or fun, or something you've been struggling with, in your personal life over the past week?*

This question is meant to help people open up and share a little bit about what brings them joy in their personal lives or share a struggle with the team that can help make them more relatable. People tend to connect when they either enjoy the same things or can relate to similar struggles.

2. *What big wins happened in the business over the past week that we should acknowledge and celebrate?* This question is intended to get people to improve on how they celebrate success and establish a culture of celebrating wins.

3. *What was your biggest frustration this past week, and should we work through it as a team to ensure it doesn't continue happening?* The idea behind this question goes back to firefighting. One of the reasons we fight so many fires is that once we put out the fire, we often don't go back and try to understand why the fire started in the first place. We rarely, if ever, try to understand how to improve a process, a training segment, or a people issue so that it never happens for the same reason again going forward. (Note: Answers to this question should be added to an issues list that you can address later in the meeting.)

Action Item Review *(Five Minutes)*

Action Items are things that need to get done in a one- or at most two-week time frame. Typically, they are created as the solution to, or the first step in a solution to, solving an issue. We will get into this more when we get to the section in the agenda on issues resolution. Action Items are owned by a specific team member and have a specific due date. This five-minute section is just used to confirm that everything is getting done on time to keep us moving forward and making things happen.

If Action Items are not getting done by the due date, then there is an issue that the team needs to work through. We suggest creating an issue on your issues list when this is the case and addressing it during the appropriate part of the meeting. Use the Action Item Review section to create a strong sense of accountability to each other to get things done.

Scorecard Review *(Five Minutes)*

During the Scorecard Review, you simply go through each line of the team's scorecard, state what is being measured, what the goal for the week was, and what the actual result was. If the result for the week meets or exceeds the goal, keep going. If the goal for the week was missed, add that item to your issues list to address later in the meeting.

You want to be careful not to spend too much time getting into an off-track number during the review. You might end up spending thirty minutes going down a rabbit hole on one number and then run out of time when you get to Issues Resolution, only to realize you spent all that time on something that was not the most important thing for you to have been spending your time on.

The Scorecard Review really helps you to see whether or not, as a team, you won your prior week. This is like a sports team going into the locker room at halftime, evaluating their statistics, and working together to make adjustments so they can go out and win the next half. Think of every Weekly Tactical Meeting as your "halftime," and spend it evaluating how your team is performing and making adjustments to set yourselves up to win.

Rock Review *(Five Minutes)*

In the Rock Review, you simply have each team member quickly state the Rock or Rocks they're working on, share their list of milestones to show the team that their milestones are on track, and if they are, go to the next person or Rock. If somebody has fallen behind on their milestones, add it to your issues list to resolve and help them get back on track during the soon-to-come Issues Resolution portion of the meeting.

Another technique some of our teams prefer is to have the person start by reading their Rock out loud. In the example earlier in this chapter, they would say, "The Next Level Accountability Chart, with a clear Mission, Most Critical Outcome, and Obsessions®, is documented for every position in my reporting structure and agreed to by the leadership team." Then, they simply tell the team what they did over the last week to keep it moving forward and what they will do in the coming week to keep it moving forward. Following this example, they might go on to say, "Last week, I met with my team to get feedback on the last draft version of our Accountability Chart, and this week I'm making final edits and updates so I can present it back to them in our next departmental meeting."

Just that level of communication around activity creates a higher level of accountability and transparency for the team. Whatever you choose to do, remember that the transparency of the activities inside each of the Rocks helps to drive accountability and results.

Headlines and Updates *(Five Minutes)*

This section is used somewhat as a "catch-all." Sometimes, there is a headline that needs to be shared with the team, but it was not worth interrupting everyone with during the week, so park those things here to quickly address in your Weekly Tactical Meeting. Examples of a headline might be something like, "*Frank, one of our top clients, lost his mother earlier this week. We're sending flowers as a company, but for those of you who know him, you might want to send a personal note or give him a call.*"

Some of our clients use this time for updates on projects they are working on. One of our clients, a construction company, modified their agenda to make this a twenty-minute section, and their director of operations uses the time to give quick, bullet point updates on each of their open construction projects so the team is kept in the loop. Anything that feels like an issue gets added to their issues list to be discussed in more detail later.

Other clients will add subsections to Headlines and Updates depending on their business and what is valuable for them. One of our Guides works with a hospitality company, and they have a subsection they call "Magical Moments." The intention is that during this time, any quick stories of something that a team member did to create a wonderful experience for a guest could be mentioned, again establishing a sense of winning and fulfillment.

Resolving the Key Issues *(Sixty Minutes)*

Now that numbers and priorities have been reviewed, Action Items assessed, and all the Headlines and Updates have been communicated, it's time to get into the real meat of the meeting, prioritizing and resolving issues.

With your issues list in front of you, whether on a flip chart, a digital document on a display screen, or in a software product, we have found that the following seven-step process is a fantastic way to break down individual issues so they can be quickly addressed and steps to resolution defined and assigned.

Step 1: As a team, quickly prioritize the single most critical issue to resolve first (don't waste too much time here. If the team cannot decide, the meeting facilitator chooses). The following steps may feel time-consuming, but the closer you can get to the real issue, the closer you are to the ideal resolution. Practice this process as it will almost always save you time in the long run, and remember, *an issue clearly stated is an issue nearly solved.*

Step 2: The facilitator asks either, *"Whose issue is it?"* or *"Who wants to tee it up for the team?"* as appropriate. The issue is on the issues list because somebody needs something.

Step 3: The facilitator then asks the individual, *"Is this a brainstorming issue or an acute issue to solve?"*

Example: Brainstorming—Our Sales Playbook isn't working, and I'm not sure what to do about it. In this case, you're talking to the team because you need to brainstorm for solutions.

Example: Acute—Our sales team is not following our Sales Playbook. In this case, you are likely talking to a specific person because it is the sales leader's accountability to ensure the Sales Playbook is being followed.

If it is an acute issue to solve, then follow up by asking, *"Who are you talking to?"* or *"Who owns the decision?"* as appropriate. In the example above, you're talking to the sales leader.

Step 4: Facilitator asks person teeing up the issue, *"One sentence, be direct; what is the real issue?"* Note that we often get stuck talking about symptoms and not digging into the real issue, which is often a lack of process or somebody not following a process.

Step 5: Final setup question—The Facilitator asks, *"What is the outcome you want if we are going to give this time today?"* and/or *"What do you need from (person you're talking to) to get it resolved for good?"* Use a question like this, based on which is appropriate, to make sure that the person setting up the issue clarifies the desired outcome. This prevents the team from wandering off track and helps everyone stay focused on the issue at hand.

Step 6: Facilitator checks with the team for agreement that we have identified an underlying root cause and are not still at the symptom level.

Step 7: The relevant people in the meeting efficiently discuss the issue as necessary to get to a resolution—or the next step that moves you toward resolution. Determine the next steps, and create Action Items for accountability to those next steps. Include any cascading messages to people not in the room. Document the Action Items and cascading messages for your next meeting and include the due date.

Repeat the process going back to Step 1 until either your time is up or all the important issues for the week are resolved.

Conclude and Head Out Aligned *(Five Minutes)*

During the final five minutes of the meeting, do a quick recap of the Action Items that were established to help resolve the issues that were addressed. Be sure everyone is clear who is doing what and by when. Make sure team members are confident in committing to one another to meet their deadlines for the Action Items.

Finally, ask each attendee to rate the meeting. We like to recommend a scale of one to five, where each number has a specific meaning, with the goal of getting feedback from the team and insights into how to consistently improve the meeting so that everyone is finding the meetings to be a five out of five every time. Here is our recommendation of the definitions for the scoring system:

5. This was a valuable meeting. We stayed focused and were decisive. I have a clear direction forward.

4. This was a good meeting, but there are some things that can be improved, such as…
3. I know the meeting was necessary, but I did not get much out of it. I would have preferred…
2. This was not a good meeting. We were not…(fill in the details and be specific in terms of what would have made it better).
1. This was a total waste of my time because…

This feedback is important because it will allow the team and the facilitator to learn and adapt going forward, continually working to make your meetings a great and valuable experience for everyone.

DAILY HUDDLES

While the Weekly Tactical Meeting is a great starting point for leadership and management-level meetings, many organizations lack a meeting structure to involve and inform team members on the front lines. That is where Daily Huddles can often close the loop on communication flow, improving performance at the front-line level.

The concept of Daily Huddles, often referred to as daily stand-ups in some contexts, is closely associated with the Agile and Scrum methodologies, which were formalized in the software development industry in the early 2000s. However, the broader idea of daily team meetings for alignment and communication has roots in earlier management practices.

The Agile methodology, particularly Scrum, is where the term "Daily Stand-Up" or "Daily Scrum" originated. Jeff Sutherland and Ken Schwaber, who were key figures in the development of Scrum, popularized the practice. The Daily Scrum is a fifteen-minute meeting where team members quickly discuss what they did yesterday, what they plan to do today, and any obstacles they're facing.

There are five key benefits to incorporating Daily Huddles through the front lines of an organization.

1. **Alignment and Communication:** Daily Huddles ensure that everyone is on the same page, especially front-line employees who are closest to the customers and the day-to-day operations. These brief meetings allow the team to align on priorities, share important updates, and quickly address any issues. This consistent communication reduces misunderstandings and ensures that everyone is moving in the same direction.

2. **Problem-Solving and Agility:** Front-line employees often encounter challenges that need immediate attention. Daily Huddles create a structured opportunity to surface these problems early, allowing the team to address them before they escalate. This practice fosters a culture of proactive problem-solving and enables the business to be more agile in responding to daily challenges.

3. **Accountability and Focus:** By having a routine check-in, employees become more accountable for their tasks and progress. The daily rhythm keeps everyone focused on the most important tasks and prevents small issues from slipping through the cracks. This leads to more consistent execution and better overall performance.

4. **Employee Engagement:** Daily Huddles give front-line employees a voice, making them feel more connected to the business's goals and more engaged in their work. When employees see that their input is valued and acted upon, it increases morale and motivation.

5. **Building a Culture of Continuous Improvement:** The

daily cadence of these meetings reinforces a culture where continuous improvement is expected. As issues are identified and resolved quickly, the business can make incremental improvements daily, which compound in value over time.

Daily Huddles—An Example

During my time as CEO of Erath Veneer, after studying *Mastering the Rockefeller Habits* by Verne Harnish, we decided to implement Daily Huddles with our front-line production teams. We started with a very simple agenda to keep it focused and short. First shift started promptly at 7:00 a.m., and we decided we would ask first-shift employees to be clocked in by 6:45 a.m., and we would compensate them. The Daily Huddles would start at 6:50 a.m. We did the same thing for the second shift, which started at 3:30 p.m. Second-shift team members were expected to clock in by 3:15, and their Daily Huddles started promptly at 3:20. We believed that while this typically caused just over an hour of additional overtime per hourly team member, by having these Daily Huddles and getting engagement from the front lines, the marginal cost would only be a fraction of the marginal value we would gain.

The team lead or supervisor would run the Huddle, and the agenda we used was the same for every team:

- Prior Day's Results
  - ▷ The lead would report the prior day's productivity goal and the actual results for how the team did. They would then ask, "Any issues or concerns from yesterday we need to solve?"
- Today's Goal
  - ▷ The lead would share the goal for the coming shift and ask, "Are there any concerns or anything that could keep us from beating our goal?"

- Help and Support
  - ▷ Finally, to conclude the Huddle, the lead would ask, "Is there anything that anybody needs from me or anyone else before we get started?"

That's it. Every day, just before the start of every shift, every front-line team member knew whether or not they "won the day" for the prior day, they knew what they needed to do for the current day, and they knew that their lead was there to help and support them.

> For an overview of how we teach our clients to run Daily Huddles, just go to YouTube.com and type "Next Level Growth Daily Huddles" in the search bar, or visit YouTube.com/@NextLevelGrowth and find it on the playlist, "Rolling Out the Five Obsessions of Elite Organizations."

One of the first positive things that started happening when we implemented these front-line Daily Huddles is that team members who otherwise just kept their heads down and did their jobs started to become more engaged, more aware, and more proactive. One specific example I will never forget happened with the first shift team on our veneer dryer number three.

When you slice hardwood veneer, you first have to cook the logs in massive stainless-steel vats to saturate the wood fibers with moisture and heat so that the thin sheets of veneer can be sliced without tearing the fibers. On average, veneer comes off of a veneer slicer at somewhere between 70 to 75 percent moisture content, and an average log can easily produce more than one thousand sheets of veneer. To be usable, each individual sheet needs to be dried down to between 10 and 12 percent. Veneer dryers are used to dry the sheets after slicing, and the sheets have to be manually fed into the machine one sheet at a time.

Veneer dryers, depending on various factors, are anywhere from seventy-five to one hundred and twenty feet long and can have several hundred sheets of veneer in them at any given time. When there is any kind of breakdown with a veneer dryer that causes the conveyor system to stop moving, the sheets (product) inside the dryer will be overdried and usually ruined.

Joy had been feeding Dryer #3 on the first shift for several years and had been with our family business for more than two decades. We had tried to promote her to a lead position several times, but she always declined, preferring instead to have the simple security of the job she knew so well. In many ways, it is my memories of Joy that have framed my belief that you can be an A-Player and, at the same time, not be interested in a career path and developing into a leader.

Soon after we implemented Daily Huddles, Joy spoke up during the "Help and Support" portion of a brief daily huddle. All she said was that the day before, she had started hearing a noise that she had not noticed before and didn't know if something was wrong with the dryer. The meeting adjourned, and the team went to work.

Armed with this information from Joy, the Dryer #3 lead, Elaine, who was also a long-time employee and someone we all affectionately called "Red," asked the first shift supervisor to send somebody over from maintenance as soon as possible. Within a few minutes, Jeff from our maintenance crew stopped by to check on Red, who let him know what Joy had mentioned in the huddle. Jeff went to Joy's station and stood with her for a few minutes so she could point out the occasional noise she was hearing.

Jeff quickly realized that the faint sound she was hearing was the very early sign of a bearing beginning to fail. The conveyor system that operates inside a veneer dryer consists of a stainless-steel screen roughly thirteen feet wide and several hundred feet long winding its way through a series of large rollers, each turning on a shaft with roller bearings on each end. If a bearing were to fail when the veneer dryer was full of product, the machine would stop, and all of the product inside, easily worth several thousand dollars, would be ruined. If the failure was bad enough, there could also be damage to the screen, which could cost tens of thousands of dollars to repair.

Because Joy had a platform to speak up in the Daily Huddle and share that she noticed something was different, we were able to identify the bearing that was beginning to fail, allow them to run the dryer until it was empty before their lunch break, and then change the bearing during lunch, having everything back up and running by the time they came back to work. Not only did this prevent the team from losing any production that shift, it also prevented significant product damage, and possibly machine damage, from happening.

Never underestimate the power and value of getting your front-line team members engaged and speaking up. They are so much closer to what is really going on that management can gain incredible insights just by giving them a platform to share their concerns and be heard.

AN A-PLAYER SYSTEM TO IMPROVE INDIVIDUAL PERFORMANCE

While the systems and structures mentioned above, from Scorecards and Scoreboards to Growth Rocks, Weekly Tactical Meetings, and Daily Huddles, will help optimize team performance, there are two additional systems that we teach our clients to help them custom-tailor the way individuals are coached and developed. They are *Quarterly Calibrations* and a *Coaching System.*

Every great performer has a coach. Many of them have multiple coaches. In fact, most professional golfers on the PGA Tour will work with a Swing Coach, a Mental Coach, a Fitness and Strength Coach, and a Nutrition Coach. These players are the best of the best, and even so, they are obsessed with coaching and feedback in order to be at their very best.[25] What is your organization doing to develop your leaders into great coaches?

> "What a leader has to do is define an environment in which everyone can excel. You have to create capacity in others. There has to be something in it for your people. You have to give them a vision of the capability you see in them and the good that will come for them as a result of their efforts. When you do this, people are much more likely to listen to you and bring their best to the work that they do."[26]
>
> —DR. NIDO QUBEIN

At Next Level Growth, we recommend that everyone who has direct reports be developed by the organization to be a coach for their teams. As part of that coaching system, we recommend what we call *Quarterly Calibrations.* These are one-to-one meetings, once per quarter, between a leader and each of their direct reports, where they discuss core values one at a time and then performance relative to the defined Mission,

25 John Berardi, "The 6 Pillars of Training for Golf with Dr. Greg Wells," Precision Nutrition, accessed December 5, 2024, https://www.precisionnutrition.com/6-pillars-training-golf.

26 Nido Qubein, interview by the author, October 14, 2024.

Most Critical Outcome, and Obsessions (MMOs) from the Next Level Accountability Chart, again, each one at a time.

We also recommend clarifying and utilizing a numeric rating system, with definitions for each of the numbers relative to expectations for both behavior relative to each core value and performance relative to each part of the MMOs. We prefer starting with one of three simple designations for each individual item: the team member is exceeding expectations, the team member is meeting expectations, or the team member is not meeting expectations. We have some clients who choose to use a one-to-three scoring system, some who use a one-to-five system, and others who use a one-to-ten system, and each of their rating systems creates a relative scale within those three designations. All that really matters is that the system is clear, it is consistently deployed throughout the organization, and the meaning of the numbers is defined.

When this is consistently done every quarter throughout the organization, you are validating with your high achievers that they are doing well, and you are identifying your underperformers so that you can work with them to understand their needs and help develop and coach them up. If, however, over time, you find that somebody is not responding to or accepting the coaching, then you can either coach them into another seat or coach them out of the organization as appropriate. This makes room for a new recruit to come through your onboarding processes and refill the seat with an expectation that the new, well-onboarded recruit will be able to perform at a higher level.

QUARTERLY CALIBRATIONS

Most relatively complex pieces of equipment, like a watch, a machine, or an engine, need to be periodically calibrated in order to maintain optimal performance. People are no different.

Leticia Gastelum, chief people officer for GradGuard®, a fast-growing company that is the leading provider of tuition and renter's insurance in the country, helping students and families protect their investment in higher education, helped us coin the phrase "Quarterly Calibrations." Until Leticia joined GradGuard in January of 2024, we had been referring to the quarterly check-ins between leaders and their team members as Quarterly Coaching Conversations. It was Leticia who challenged the wording and, after learning the how and why behind what we were teaching, suggested that they were more like a calibration than a coaching conversation. While it seems like a small change, it was actually pretty significant.

If I look at it from the outside in, having a "coaching conversation" with my boss every quarter may sound like I need to listen and take notes. It feels one-directional. When you think of it instead as a calibration and something that is not only focused on performance but also on the working relationship I have with my boss, it feels more collaborative. The process we were teaching was, in fact, highly collaborative and relational, but the name we had chosen to give it had the potential to set an expectation that was not fully aligned with the intention of the process.

Quarterly Calibrations are intended to last somewhere between ten and thirty minutes, depending on the role and how well the person is performing in the role. They are also intended to be somewhat casual and not feel like a formal annual performance review.

The basic structure of the Quarterly Calibration is designed to provide a different conversation than bosses and employees have on a day-to-day basis and help establish clear expectations around culture, values, and performance to keep everyone on track. In a nutshell, the conversation should be scheduled in advance, usually at least a week ahead, so there is time to prepare. This also lets your direct report know you are prioritizing your time with them to the point of calendaring it. Be sure to let them know this is not a formal review but just a casual check-in conversation to make sure you're both aligned on core values, performance expectations, and any concerns they have so that you can help them succeed.

The conversation should ideally be off-site for leaders and managers, most often at a coffee shop or over breakfast or lunch, and on- or off-site at your discretion for front-line employees. Some businesses use the break room during non-break times for front-line employees. This creates a more relaxed setting than being in your office and will lead to more openness in the dialogue. Remember, you want your direct report to feel at ease and able to speak freely.

In advance of the meeting, complete an A-Player Assessment (*see image below—downloadable at FiveObsessions.com*) for the employee, just focusing on the last ninety days. Also, give the employee a blank copy of the A-Player Assessment and ask them to do a self-assessment for the same ninety-day period, using a one to ten scale, basing their rating for each on the definitions at the bottom of the form. As mentioned earlier, feel free to come up with your own scale, just make sure there are very clear definitions for what the ratings mean. Evaluate them on each of your core values individually, asking, "How consistently have their behaviors at work aligned with this core value?"

Then do the same for their Mission, MCO, and Obsessions from the Accountability Chart, asking, "How consistently have they been doing great work in that area?" Also, think about any areas where you feel they are performing well and any areas where you would like to see them focus on improving. Ask the employee to use the same process.

NEXT LEVEL GROWTH

Employee Name: _____   Date: _____

	Core Value 1	Core Value 2	Core Value 3	Core Value 4	Core Value 5	Core Value 6	Core Value 7	Core Value Score	Mission/MCO™	Obsession 1	Obsession 2	Obsession 3	Obsession 4	Obsession 5	Obsession 6	Obsession 7	Performance Score
Score:																	

Strengths and Accomplishments:

Areas Needing Improvement:

Action Items for Improving:

Employee Comments:

Sample Scoring Definitions

9–10	Significantly exceeds expectations – A Player	4–6	Generally below expectations – C Player
8–9	Generally exceeds expectations – A Player	1–3	Significantly below expectations – C Player
7	Generally meets expectations – B Player/A Potential		

Signatures:

Employee: _____   Date: _____

Evaluated by: _____   Date: _____

Witnessed by: _____   Date: _____

NextLevelGrowth.com
© 2020 Next Level Growth

Figure 6.2

Download this form and more at FiveObsessions.com

When you meet with the employee, start by checking in with them on family and personal life. Remember that part of the goal is to build a connection and relationship. Then move into core values. Take them one at a time and ask the employee how they evaluated themselves on the first core value, using the behavior question above. Listen to what they are saying and ask questions as necessary. Then share with them how you evaluated them. If you are on the same page, that's good. If anything needs to improve, or if you're misaligned, have a conversation about that. Then move to the next core value.

On a personal note, when I am having a Quarterly Calibration with any of my direct reports, I like to start by reminding them that, based on our ten-point scale, a seven is a perfectly fine score and means that they are meeting expectations. When you start the meeting and following your check-in, start by asking your direct report whether, for your first core value, they feel like they've been meeting the expectation, exceeding it, or coming up short. Oftentimes, you may never actually get into discussing each other's numbers. Just their answer to that question gets you into the conversation you need to have.

If you are not aligned, you might use the number to add clarity. For example, if the team member thinks they've been meeting an expectation and you think they've been slightly below on a few occasions, you might have given them a five or six instead of a seven. In addressing the examples of where they have missed the mark, you might let them know that while it was not too significant of a problem, you did rate them a five or six and then share the reasons why. If, on the other hand, they significantly missed the mark, you should use the lower end of the one to six scale for underperforming as a way to highlight the degree of the miss.

On the other hand, you might feel like the team member has been meeting your expectations, so for you they are a seven, but in their mind they are being too hard on themselves and rated their performance a five or six. This gives you a good opportunity to ask them why, with specific examples, they felt they were missing expectations.

For example, there may have been a few mistakes that they made which, for you, were part of a learning process and are not something you would consider underperformance. In their mind, they may be fixated on the mistake, and this allows you to ask clarifying questions about what they learned from the mistake. If it is clear that they learned what they needed to, and evolved as a result, you could explain to them that you expect them to make a few mistakes as they accept responsibility and take ownership of their role and reinforce to them that it is more about how they learned and grew through a mistake than the mistake itself. This can boost their confidence and also help them see you as a boss who is understanding and who wants to see them be decisive, as long as they are willing to learn and grow when they make a mistake.

After you've been through all of the core values, move right to the Mission, MCO, and Obsessions from the Accountability Chart. Go through exactly the same process using the question around performance. The point is to get on the same page with each other and make sure they are continuing to grow and improve.

A few other good questions to ask before you conclude are the same three I mentioned in the section of the book about onboarding in Chapter 5. I'm repeating them here to both reinforce their importance and to keep you from having to go back to a previous chapter now:

- Is there anything you need from me that you aren't getting? Resources, time, training, clear expectations, etc.?
- Is there anything going on that is frustrating you or making it difficult to work here?

- Is there anything I'm doing that is making it difficult to work for me?

Most employees never get the opportunity to have these kinds of conversations, and when they do, it creates fantastic engagement. If the process helps you identify that somebody needs to be put on a Performance Improvement Plan, let this meeting be a segue into that process to either coach them up or coach them out.

A COACHING SYSTEM FOR COACHING UP OR COACHING OUT—WHEN COACHING CONVERSATIONS AREN'T WORKING

In *Good to Great*, Jim Collins talks about the importance of a "culture of discipline," specifically about disciplined people, engaged in disciplined thought and taking disciplined action. Getting the right people on the bus, the wrong people off the bus, and the right people in the right seats. Simple, right? Just because it's simple does not mean it is easy.

People's underperformance is one of the toughest issues for any leadership team to solve. Whether there are emotional attachments, nepotism, long history, unique circumstances, hidden secrets, or any other reasons, it is challenging to have difficult conversations about specific people and their underperformance or fit with your culture. Regardless of the difficulty, you need to address the issues and do so with names rather than just complaining about "some people". You must take formal action to protect the company—or even let those people go if that is the right thing to do.

Making "people decisions" very often comes down to cultural fit, performance to expectations, or both. People who don't fit the company's defined culture are Right People (RP) issues. Clear core values and the organization's Purpose become the language that separates those who belong to the tribe and those who don't. Those who do not live up to the company's performance standards are Right Seat (RS) issues. The Next Level Accountability Chart defines each seat based on outcomes and results around how the seat creates value. Does the person in the seat have the aptitude, skills, and desire to consistently perform at a high level? Sometimes the person is not the Right Person *and also* is not in the Right Seat, which is a Right Person, Right Seat (RPRS) issue.

Leadership teams often get bogged down in and distracted by stories about people and their underperformance or lack of cultural fit. There will be reasons, excuses, rationalizations, and explanations for why someone does not fit the culture, meet performance standards, or both. Ultimately, things pay off on results, not effort, so when you have an issue with a team member failing to meet expectations, it requires you to take action.

The leadership team is responsible for everything in the organization. You have a choice to make about what you will actually do about every situation. Your job as a leadership team is to make decisions. You must generate viable, relevant decisions to your issues as quickly as possible for the greater good of the organization. The Coaching System is designed to cut through the noise and clutter and put the focus on what to do next for the benefit of the person, the team, the department, and the company as a whole.

When you have an underperforming employee or one who does not feel like a good culture fit, you need to use a process to either coach them up or coach them out. We always recommend that, unless the circumstances are to an extreme that requires immediate write-up or termination, start with one or two Coaching Conversations. Unlike Calibrations, these are more of a one-sided delivery of clarity about what is expected, citation of specific examples where the employee missed the mark, and clarification of and agreement to what must change going forward to get back on track. You can use the same form from the Quarterly Calibrations for this process if you find it helpful.

What you must avoid is the trap of getting into endless Coaching Conversations without getting the positive momentum you need to see from the team member. I've seen far too many leaders complain about the same person over and over, and then default to say, "I'm working with them and coaching them," even though it has been going on for multiple quarters. The following corrective action process is a highly effective approach to use if one or two Coaching Conversations have not worked. This process takes the emotion and subjectivity out of solving difficult people issues. Here's how it works. We call these Coaching Plans, something you may have heard referred to as a corrective action plan (CAP) or performance improvement plan (PIP). To reinforce the idea that leaders are coaches and that the goal is a positive outcome, we prefer the term *Coaching Plan*.

Preparation

1. Use the A-Player Performance Review document to determine where the issue or issues are with the person. Is it a core values issue, a performance issue, or both? (Note: downloadable at FiveObsessions.com)
2. Be sure to have a witness in the meeting, as this is a formal process that may lead to termination, so you need to make sure you cover your bases just in case.
3. For each of the areas where there is an issue, do your best to come up with three examples in recent memory (not more than about ninety days, or not since the last meeting once you get past the First Meeting, described below) to support your evaluation and add them to the appropriate section of the Performance Review. Most people will excuse

one example as an outlier if one example is all you have. If they're a good negotiator, they might try to talk you out of two examples. However, if you have three recent examples, most people will acquiesce and stop pushing back.

The Meetings

First Meeting

- Be firm but supportive, clear, and direct.
- Go over the A-Player Assessment with the team member one item at a time, complimenting them on where they are doing well and getting clear with them on where they are not. Ensure that they understand you and ask them what you can expect to see from them in the coming days and weeks that will resolve your concerns. Do this for each specific area where they are not meeting your expectations.
- Note their feedback in the "Action Items for Improving" section of the form, and coach them as needed through developing those strategies.
- You, the employee, and the witness all sign the form, and you schedule the Second Meeting—usually two to four weeks out—before you conclude the First Meeting. No matter what, you have the Second Meeting.

Second Meeting

Follow the same preparation steps as the First Meeting. Be positive and appreciative if they've improved, and increasingly firm and direct if not:

- Go over the A-Player Assessment with the team member one item at a time, just as before.

- ▷ If the employee has improved and you are satisfied, thank them for their efforts, and keep an eye on them to be sure they don't slip back into old ways. All three people sign the document, it goes in their HR file, and you do not need to have any further meetings as the problem, for now, is resolved.
- ▷ If the employee is still not meeting expectations, work together and note Action Items on the form that are required to get them performing by the next meeting. You, the employee, and the witness all sign the form, and it goes in their HR file.
- If a Third Meeting is required, schedule it before you conclude the Second Meeting—again, usually two to four weeks out—and this time, you clearly advise the team member that if they are not meeting your expectations by the Third Meeting, it will be their exit interview. No matter what, you have the Third Meeting.

Third Meeting

Follow the same preparation steps as the first two meetings. One of three things will have happened since the Second Meeting:

1. The team member got it in gear and is no longer an issue. Start the meeting by congratulating them so they know they are not getting fired, then go over a plan to stay on track going forward so they don't backslide. Document the conversations as necessary, have everyone sign the document, and keep an eye on things going forward.
2. The team member did not make the necessary improvements, and this is their exit interview. Be kind and direct. Start by letting them know you've got bad news and this is going to be their last day with the company. Have

the Assessment filled out, quickly let them know the areas where they are still underperforming, and ask them to sign the form (note that they may refuse.) Ironically in these cases, most employees know they are being fired and have already started looking for something else. Many of them will appreciate the chances and your honesty with them over the course of the meetings. Others will act out.[27]

3. Most often, the meeting is not necessary because the team member left on their own rather than waiting around to be fired. In this case, they are no longer your HR concern, and the issue solved itself.

Many leaders are hesitant to take corrective action, usually because of the formality. Please understand the formality of the process is the power behind it (hence, scheduled meetings, paperwork, etc.). Follow your process, and keep in mind that if you—as their leader—want it more for them than they want it for themselves, it will never work out. The effort is their responsibility, not yours.

Remember, people issues are the toughest issues that leaders and managers face, which is why the *Great People* obsession comes first. Every company is a collection of unique people and processes, designed to deliver on the organization's core business with consistency, reliability, and efficiency. Many people issues are fraught with danger because of "either/or" thinking: Either we keep them and continue to suffer, or we suffer through firing them. This disempowering context stops our movement, creating indecision and fear that saps energy from the organization.

---

27 Disclaimer: We are not employment lawyers and suggest you consult one. We have had this process evaluated by HR professionals in multiple states, including California, and everyone agrees that this process gives employees cause for termination, gives them opportunities to improve in order to prevent termination, and gives them time to make the necessary improvements to avoid termination. By doing this, you will likely put yourself and the organization in a very strong position to defend any claims of wrongful termination.

Your leadership team runs your business. You will get what you're willing to tolerate. If someone stands in between your leadership team and doing what's best for the company, then that person runs your business. Think about that. Who runs your organization? Who determines what is possible or impossible as you move toward your Summit? I hope that this A-Player System makes it easier for you to move through these complex people issues as part of your obsession around *Great People*, and truly take your business to the *Next Level*.

Never Settle—Have Clear Expectations

As I wrote earlier, I believe that most of our frustrations with people are rooted in *unclear expectations*. The Next Level Accountability Chart is a great tool to help clarify the performance expectations of people in their roles. Once those expectations are clear, and you use them in the recruiting, hiring, onboarding, and continuous development phases of your employee journey, you will have the foundation of a system that is designed to help you drive performance from a team of *Great People*.

As Nick Saban, one of the most successful football coaches of all time, has often said, "Mediocre people don't like high achievers, and high achievers don't like mediocre people."[28] If you don't have a *Culture of Performance*, one where everyone has bought into the same expectations and the same high standards, you cannot have any team chemistry within the organization. You must have clear expectations if you are going to have a high performing culture.

In the end, a *Culture of Performance* is a commitment across the organization, starting with leadership, to the same high expectations around achieving results. You must commit to providing your team with the right strategy to become a dominant force in your space, use

---

28 Saban, "Nick Saban and the Mindset of Great People."

an A-Player Recruiting and Onboarding System, set Clear Expectations, leverage Scorecards and Scoreboards, and follow a Coaching System to both keep your high performers at their peak, and coach underperformers up or out as necessary.

You cannot be elite if you are content with being good.

For more assistance in building out your own *Culture of Performance*, don't forget that you can consult with **AskMichael Erath.com** for lots of interaction and deeper conversations about how to customize this, and the rest of our framework, for your unique circumstances.

With your organization full of *Great People*, aligned and driven by an *Inspiring Purpose*, with *Optimized Playbooks* and a *Culture of Performance*, you have to be intentional about *Growing Profits and Cash Flow*, the lifeblood of your organization, and the fifth of the Five Obsessions of Elite Organizations.

Chapter 7

OBSESSION #5: GROWING PROFITS AND CASH FLOW

"Profit and cash flow are like oxygen.
You don't realize how much you need them
until suddenly, you don't have them."

—widely attributed to MICHAEL GERBER

THE IMPORTANCE OF RESILIENCE— A PERSONAL LESSON LEARNED

When the terrorist attacks happened on September 11, 2001, I was thirty years old and the president and CEO of Erath Veneer. By that time, about 80 percent of our business was export, primarily to Europe and Asia. Our customers would typically travel to the US every two or three months to inspect and purchase products from us.

Even though the closure of airspace in North America lasted only two days, it took six to nine months before our overseas customers began to return to travel. Many of them were distributors, and they had large inventories and low overheads, so they survived off of their inventories during the global economic downturn that followed. We, on the other hand, were a manufacturer, with significant fixed cost structures and debt service.

Our sales dropped an average of 60 percent in the two quarters following the attacks, and we quickly ran dangerously low on cash. In my youth, I was aggressively growing the business, focusing on opening new markets and expanding capacity, but I wasn't intentional about simultaneously building a war chest of cash reserves and assuring sufficient access to capital, so our balance sheet was not in the position to easily weather such a storm.

While we did survive and go on to begin growing again, it would not be until two years later, when I joined YPO, that I would begin to really learn and understand the tools and concepts I needed in order to build a more resilient company. Many of those tools and concepts provide the framework for the fifth of the Five Obsessions, *Growing Profit and Cash Flow.*

> To read more about Michael's own entrepreneurial journey, a journey filled with successes, failures, and a business partner's embezzlement, fraud, felony conviction, and eventual federal prison time, followed by Michael's rebirth from the ashes of it all, read or listen to his 2017 bestselling book, *RISE: The Reincarnation of an Entrepreneur.* A journey about which well-known author and founder of the COO Alliance, Cameron Herold, says, "I've met countless entrepreneurs over the course of my two-plus decades in business. Few have stories as dramatic—and, in the end, as inspirational—as Michael Erath's." You can purchase the book or audiobook by visiting NextLevelGrowth.com/Books.[29]

---

29 Erath, *RISE.*

Over the course of my career as both an owner of multiple businesses and now a mentor and Business Guide to many more, I have seen how many entrepreneurs, and even many business operating systems, view profit and cash flow as the result of getting everything else right. While in theory, that thought process makes sense, I believe that to truly build an elite organization, the entire premise on which Next Level Growth was created and differentiates itself, you must be intentional and proactive about *Growing Profits and Cash Flow*.

In this chapter, I will take you through five disciplines and concepts that you can begin to implement right away, and which will also help you improve both your profitability and your net cash flow quickly. They are:

- Internal Financial Literacy
- Profit per X
- Cash Conversion Cycles
- Cash Flow Forecasting
- The Power of Incremental Change

INTERNAL FINANCIAL LITERACY

Many business owners are reluctant to share financial statements and other measures of financial performance with their leadership teams out of a fear that the people around them will get distracted or greedy if they know the profitability of the company when things are good. They might also fear that key employees will get scared away knowing how much the company may be losing when times are bad. I would argue, however, that if an entrepreneur surrounds themselves with leaders who do not have either the financial understanding of or the appreciation for the risks the entrepreneur is taking and often personally liable for, then they have the wrong leaders sitting around the table.

For much of my early career, I was also one of those entrepreneurs who concealed financial statements from everyone other than my controller. It wasn't until I hired my first true CFO, and also through continuing to read and learn about best practices from my YPO colleagues and authors like Jack Stack, that I began to come around. I eventually created a monthly financial review meeting with my leadership team that was transformational in opening their eyes to understanding how decisions they and their teams were making had a broader impact on the company. It also allowed me to delegate the burden of being the only one who carried the stress of the financial roller coaster on which entrepreneurial organizations often ride.

I even came up with an exercise that I began doing with supervisors and lower-level employees to help them better understand that the dollar amounts we sold were far from the dollar amounts that the company, and in turn, I, as its shareholder, actually made.

The Relatability of a One-Hundred-Dollar Bill

At Next Level Growth, we have an image of a one-hundred-dollar bill that has been resized so it prints exactly ten inches wide, which makes it easy to divide accurately every time we use this exercise. We share it regularly with many of our clients, and you can also see a video of the exercise on our YouTube channel in the "No Fluff, No Theory: Just Hard-Hitting Business Lessons" playlist at YouTube.com/ @NextLevelGrowth.

I first came up with this exercise when I was running my second manufacturing business, and I started by printing off the image and cutting away the excess paper, so that it looks just like an oversized one-hundred-dollar bill on the front side and is blank paper on the back. Then, using a ruler, I mark the back of the bill based on the primary categories from our financial statements. Because we were a manufacturing business, our cost of goods sold (COGS) was 70 percent of sales and was made up of four categories: direct materials cost, freight in (getting those materials shipped to our facility), direct manufacturing cost, and direct labor.

In an average year, we spent approximately 35 percent of our revenue on materials, another 5 percent on freight in, around 20 percent on direct manufacturing costs, and 10 percent on direct labor to prepare finished goods for sale. Based on those percentages, I measured from one end of the bill three and a half inches, representing the 35 percent materials cost, and drew a vertical line. Then, I measured another half inch and drew another vertical line. From there, I measured two more inches to represent the direct manufacturing cost and drew another line. Finally, I measured another inch and drew a vertical line to represent our direct labor cost. That left me with only three remaining inches of the one-hundred-dollar bill, each mark representing the portion of that bill that was spent on each of the various categories.

Next came our operating expenses, all of the remaining costs of running the business that were not directly related to producing goods for sale. That expense, on average, ran about 10 percent, so I marked off another inch on the back of the bill. Depending on revenue, our remaining overheads and General and Administrative expenses (G&A) were between 12 and 13 percent of revenue, so I marked off another one and a quarter inches. The hardwood veneer business had become very commoditized, with significant cheap import competition from Asian countries and primarily from China, so if we were able to earn a Net Income of around 7 percent, we were happy.

With the bill properly marked, I would meet with teams of employees and, only showing them the face of the bill, explain to them that for every one hundred dollars we sold to a customer, we had to spend on average thirty-five of those dollars on the logs, and I would take the scissors and cut away the first 35 percent of the bill. Then I would explain that we had to pay trucking companies to haul the logs to us, and I cut away another 5 percent.

I then would explain that we had to pay to have the logs produced into veneer, and that cost another twenty dollars of every hundred, so I cut away another 20 percent. Finally, I explained that all of our employees who were involved in preparing products for sale cost another ten dollars for every hundred, so I cut off another 10 percent. At this point, there was only 30 percent of the one-hundred-dollar bill left. They were beginning to understand.

What many of them did not realize was that we had to pay for our logs before they could be shipped, and we had to pay for the manufacturing costs, freight, and employee payroll as production was happening, so before we sold anything to our customers, we had to have money to invest in paying those bills. Many of them had not understood how much cash it took, and tied up, to have goods produced and in the warehouse ready to be sold.

From there, I explained that we had other operating expenses, like office rent, insurance, non-sales-related travel, training for non-production employees, and licenses and fees for technology products, and I cut away another 10 percent. Finally, I explained what made up G&A, and cut away another inch and a quarter. There I stood with less than one inch of the bill remaining. Everyone understood, and almost all of them were surprised. While I didn't get into the nuance of a C corporation versus an S corporation, I simply said, "Don't forget, the government is going to be sure they get theirs," and I cut away a third of what little was left of the bill.

I now stood before them with barely half an inch left of the one-hundred-dollar bill, representing about 6 percent of what I started with. I asked the team, "Do you think we should be reinvesting in the business each year so that we have nice equipment and can continue providing a good environment for everyone?" The answer was a resounding yes, so I cut the remaining sliver in half.

There I stood, with only three one-hundredths of a one-hundred-dollar bill left in my fingers. Everyone understood. Then I said something that really got their attention. *"This is all that is left if, and only if, everybody does their job well. If someone makes a mistake and ruins one of our logs, we have to replace it."* I picked up the three-and-a-half-inch piece of paper that represented the log cost and asked them, *"Where does the money for this come from if we have to replace the log?"* Tony, our warehouse supervisor, said, *"I guess that has to come from you?"*

"Exactly," I said. *"I do if the company is tight on cash, or the company does if we have the cash. Somebody has to dig into their pockets to pay to replace the log and replace the freight to get it here. And that's either the business or me."* I went on to facilitate a conversation with them about the importance of staying focused on quality and being careful not to get sloppy because for the company to be profitable, a requirement for them to get paid and have job security, we could not afford to make careless mistakes.

Taking the time to share that analogy had a fantastic impact on employee engagement and morale. Many of them, especially the front-line manufacturing employees, never had anyone teach them about personal finance, much less about how finances work in a business. Keeping it simple with the hundred-dollar bill presented the information in a context that was easy to understand and relate to. All of them could relate to a hundred dollars. If I had used real financials and spreadsheets, and lots of big numbers, they would have been lost.

Consider doing this exercise with your own teams to help them better understand and engage with the organization's need to grow profits and cash flow.

Monthly Financial Review: A Best Practice Recommendation

As I evolved as a leader, I worked with our controller to create a spreadsheet to which we would export a budget to an actual variance analysis report from our financial software as soon as the months were closed. This report listed each month what our budget (or forecast for those of you who prefer forecasts to budgets) predicted and what our actual results were, and then showed the variance. Every line item on the financial report, and this was a detailed, not consolidated version, had the name of a leadership team member next to it based on who within our Next Level Accountability Chart was ultimately accountable for that line item.

Any line items that were outside of a predetermined range in terms of their actual results from what was budgeted would be highlighted in yellow. This report was distributed to the leadership team as soon as it was ready, and the following week, we would add thirty minutes to our Weekly Tactical Meeting and start with a financial review. For any line item highlighted in yellow, the leadership team member who was accountable for that line was expected to be prepared to present an update to the team.

Notice that I didn't say we just highlighted items that missed the budget. We highlighted everything that was outside of a predetermined range. If a number was off budget in a negative way, the leadership team member accountable was expected to present to the team on specifically why the number was off, what was being done to correct it going forward, and anywhere they were stuck and needed help.

Conversely, if the number beat budget, meaning it was off track to the good, they were expected to also present on specifically why they were able to beat budget, what they learned as a result, and how they were going to adjust systems, Process Playbooks, people, etc., going forward in order to systemize what they had learned and capture as much upside as possible.

That second part is very important.

> As dangerous as it is to not understand why you are underperforming, it is also dangerous to achieve successes and not clearly understand why.

In addition to the Profit and Loss statement review through the budget to actual variance report analysis, we would also review our Statement of Cash Flow on a monthly basis. Combining this with the financial review helped our team understand how much cash was increasing or decreasing based on operations, financing activities, and investing activities. The more they understood the connection between decisions in the field and the financial impacts on the business, both in terms of profit and net cash flow, the more equipped they were to make intelligent and informed decisions on a daily basis and the more autonomy they gained in their roles.

It didn't take long before our leadership team members, as soon as they received the monthly spreadsheet, would do things like go to our finance team and ask for a printout of the general ledger for lines that were off track and for which they were accountable. Over time, it created a powerful collaboration between the finance team and the rest of the leaders in the organization. This collaboration would make all of us smarter and more aligned as a team, which would benefit the organization greatly.

Another positive impact that came from this practice is that instead of being the only one focused on our financial performance and thinking about the inputs and outputs and how to best manage them, I now had a team of people, all with diverse opinions and different perspectives, ideas, and skill sets, working with me and helping me carry the burden. It was a very freeing place to be.

A Clear Picture Creates Clear Decisions

One of our former clients is a small professional services firm in Southern California. They started working with us after having two back-to-back strong and profitable years, followed by a year where they suddenly lost money. They had been talking with one of our Partners and Business Guides about working together for more than three years before they finally decided to engage. Instead of engaging when the business was profitable and growing, a time when we could have helped them systemize and safeguard many things, it took the shock of going from two years of nearly 20 percent profits to a year of loss to get them to make a move.

The founder, a highly creative visionary, had always relied on an outside CPA to review his financials with him. He had a bookkeeper on staff, but he didn't have anyone inside the company who could keep a sharp eye on their financials from an analytical perspective, and being a very right-brained creative, it simply was not an area of expertise or interest for him. The problem with relying on his CPA was that his CPA was only looking at the financials for accuracy, not for analysis and optimization.

His leadership team worked together with their Guide for a few months, and reluctantly, the founder soon after came to their Guide and said things were getting so bad financially that he had to end their engagement and that he and his partner were putting a hold on paying themselves. Things were really bad. Over the years, the founder and our Guide had built a good friendship, so the Guide offered to get into his financials with him as a personal favor if he would be willing to work together after hours. He wanted to see if he could help him get any clarity into what was going on and what he needed to do to stop the bleeding. The founder enthusiastically agreed.

Our Guide asked him to send over five consecutive years of detailed financial statements, which included their two best years. He then transferred each statement into a spreadsheet, creating one column for each year, and then created five additional columns to calculate every line item, for each individual year, but to show that line item for the given year as a percentage of Gross Profit.

> Note: The way their business operates, they don't account for COGS, so their Gross Profit and Revenue are the same number.

One thing that is worth mentioning here has to do with an often-erroneous focus on Revenue over Gross Profit. If you really want to be efficient financially, we believe you should look at every line item below Gross Profit as a percentage not of Revenue dollars, but of Gross Profit dollars. Primarily G&A and operating expenses. Any dollars the business is spending that you cannot justify through the lens of how many dollars of Gross Profit that expenditure will return, is potentially wasteful. That is not to say it *is* wasteful, but that it is potentially wasteful. There should be a strategic reason for the expense if it is not driving Gross Profit dollars.

In reviewing the spreadsheet their Guide had created to analyze their best years and compare those to their prior years (especially 2022 and

2023) and to their current year to date (2024) there was one line that jumped off the spreadsheet: Total Payroll Expense.

From 2021 to 2022, their Revenue had skyrocketed 62 percent and 2022 was their most profitable year of the previous five. They executed the additional work in 2022 while spending 38.5 percent of their Gross Profit dollars on labor. Said another way, every $38.50 they spent on labor returned them $100 of Gross Profit. Their Net Income that year was just over 23 percent.

As often happens with entrepreneurs, when times are good and the business is growing, there is a sense that the trend will magically continue and that they need to staff up to be ready. In this case, the company did just that, including hiring a very expensive and very qualified team member who had over three decades of experience in their industry and had even owned his own business. His hiring came with lots of promises of what he could do and all the work he could win for the firm. The partners were excited about the possibilities.

Revenue for 2023 was flat to 2022, but Payroll Expenses went up from 38.5 percent to 43 percent. While that may not feel like a huge jump, it means that for every one hundred dollars of Gross Profit they earned, they were spending an extra $4.50 to get it, which, as a percentage, was a 12 percent increase in one year. Still, the company made money at the end of the year, and nobody was looking at the numbers to this degree, so they pressed forward.

The founder decided since the last few years had been good ones, he would also raise their base salaries. Instead of raising them enough to keep up with inflation, he raised his salary relative to the company's profitability rather than keeping his base more reasonable and taking additional compensation as draws against profits. The company was getting bloated and fat.

In 2024, with the combination of high inflation and thirteen interest rate hikes from March of 2022 through July of 2024, the business began to slow. The slowdown had started from 2022 to 2023 when they went from over 60 percent growth to flat, but they weren't analyzing their financials, and they didn't see the trends and coming challenges. Annualizing their 2024 year-to-date numbers showed that their Revenue would be down roughly 40 percent from the prior year, and as of the time the founder sent their financial statements, they had not yet started to address Payroll. No wonder the company was running out of cash and had to end the engagement at a time they desperately needed a Business Guide in their corner.

The new hire they made a few years earlier, while full of promises and always working on "something that was about to come in," had not produced any new Revenue in nearly three years, but he was very convincing and had managed to find ways to justify his continued presence and compensation. Based on the analysis, and the projections for 2024, they were now spending over 68 percent of their Gross Profit on Payroll. Again, said another way, where it cost them $38.50 on Payroll to get $100 of Gross Profit in 2022, it was now costing them over $68. That is an increase of 77 percent from 2022 to 2024.

Armed with this analysis and data, our Guide met with the founder for coffee to review and discuss the findings. His biggest concern for the company was that in an industry which needs low to moderate inflation and interest rates to thrive, if he didn't make hard decisions fast, the founder may not be able to stop the bleeding in time to save the business. As they walked through what the Guide had found, everything became very clear. The founder decided, right there in the meeting, to cut his own compensation to pre-2022 levels and to stop falling for the unproductive and expensive team member's storytelling. He would offer him either a commission-based compensation plan or a transition out of the business.

Those two moves alone should get the company to a place where they will stop bleeding cash even if the market doesn't pick up for them in the near term. While we do hope that this company will find their way back to us as a client one day, the example underscores the fact that you must be proactive and focused on financial literacy and *Growing Profits and Cash Flow* if you are going to have any chance at building something elite.

Profit per X

In Chapter 2, I mentioned Jim Collins's concept of Profit per X from his 2001 book, *Good to Great*, and shared how I became fascinated with the concept and with learning how to utilize it in our analysis of decisions we made as a business. One thing that helped me ultimately discover our Profit per X was to look at it through the lens of constraints. In the management philosophy Theory of Constraints, you look for your most significant limiting factors (constraints or bottlenecks) and work to eliminate them to improve productivity and efficiency. In following that process, I came to our most significant limiting factor that would have required significant capital investment to overcome, and so I began to focus on that as the denominator in our Profit per X.

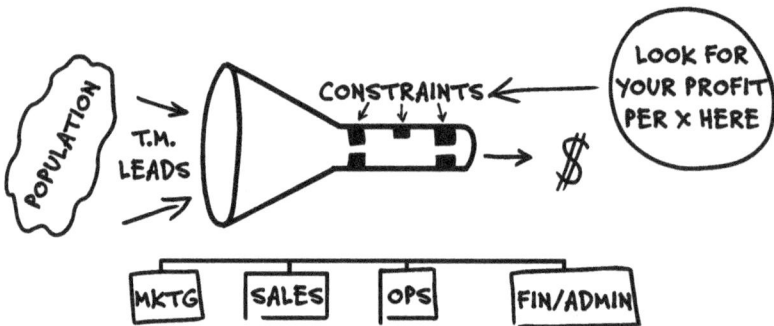

Figure 7.1

If you think of your organization as a sideways funnel, you have to extract target market leads from some population of possible leads, convert those leads to customers or clients, create and provide goods or services, and you have to get paid. Somewhere in that funnel, every organization has a single most critical constraint, or key choke point, that holds the key to driving their economic engine through a focus on Profit per X. Note that every organization has more than one, but to get the greatest impact and not get distracted, you must choose one and only one, that will have the greatest impact on your economic engine and cannot be solved by simply improving a process.

In the case of our manufacturing business, our biggest constraint was our production capacity. We were a smaller player in a big industry, and the cost of adding just one new production line would be around five million dollars, and that is just for the equipment. That doesn't include building expansion, installation costs, and startup costs. Growing our profit by physically expanding our production capacity was cost-prohibitive.

At the same time, most of our operating expenses (OpEx) and General and Administrative Expenses (G&A) were largely fixed costs. We knew that until we generated enough dollars of Gross Profit to cover those heavily fixed OpEx and G&A costs, we would not reach profitability. That was what we referred to as our "monthly nut," the amount of Gross Profit dollars it would take us just to reach breakeven for the month.

Armed with that knowledge and thinking about Profit per X in terms of constraints, we soon realized that if we could analyze and consistently make decisions to improve our dollars of Gross Profit per board foot produced (board feet is a standard unit of measure in the hardwood industry), then we could absolutely build a strong economic engine. We wrote our Profit per X as "$GP/BF" and it became everything to us.

Discovery Is Only the First Step—The Gold Is in the Analysis and Adjustments

We analyzed and then adjusted our production mix and changed our sales strategies to focus on species (think product lines) that would help us improve our $GP/BF. We analyzed and ranked all of our buyers in the field by $GP/BF for each specie we produced. Based on that data, we adjusted their budgets and quotas by specie based on their individual performance so that our highest performers relative to their $GP/BF were focused on the species where they performed best. We implemented bonus plans for the high performers to share in their profitability.

We analyzed our suppliers by specie based on $GP/BF, shared that information with our procurement team, and made adjustments to maximize our volume purchased from the highest-performing vendors. We analyzed and prioritized our customers the same way. With a finite inventory from which to sell, we looked at, by specie, which customers had the highest $GP/BF and we adjusted our sales efforts to prioritize those at the top.

Over the course of just a few quarters, as all of our analysis and adjustments began to pay off, we saw an average monthly gain in Gross Profit of just over $100,000. We achieved that without any capital expenditures and without spending any additional operating expense, which meant that essentially every dollar of additional Gross Profit fell to the bottom line and improved our profitability and net cash flow. It was worth more than $1,000,000 of additional profit and cash flow annually.

Another company we work with at Next Level Growth is an architectural firm. In their case, as a professional services firm, their most significant restraint is people, and it is the largest line item on their financials. This is the kind of organization where I've seen lots of coaches suggest tracking profit per employee, and I think that totally misses the mark. Different employees come at different price points and pay structures and produce different economic outcomes. If you think you have solved for your Profit per X with Profit per Employee, you're wrong. If you worked with a coach who told you that was it, they were wrong.

When fully burdened payroll is considered for the denominator in your Profit per X, you will get a much more accurate lens for analysis. While not consistent with GAAP accounting, for this exercise we prefer to move direct labor below the Gross Profit line so we are looking at total human capital dollars against the Gross Profit dollars with human capital removed from cost of goods sold. For the numerator, you have to answer the question, what are you investing your fully burdened payroll dollars to go get? How do you look at Return on Investment for those dollars spent? If you think it is revenue, think again. I would argue that every dollar you spend on human capital, payroll, benefits, and associated taxes, is an investment you are making that needs to produce Gross Profit dollars. I would suggest, as in the case of our architecture client, that your Profit per X in this case should be:

$$\frac{\text{Gross Profit Dollars}}{\text{Fully Burdened Payroll Dollar}}$$

or

GP$/FBP$

> Note: If in your business you are able to perform a detailed analysis of either Net Operating Income or Net Income per fully burdened human capital dollar, by product line, service line, or project, that will be even better.

Once you have your Profit per X, run a calculation looking back at your last few years' financial statements. What was the ratio in your best years and what was it in your worst years? What is it currently running year to date? That ratio should become something you report on monthly, and we would suggest (depending on your sales and billing cycles) looking at the month-to-month, quarter-to-quarter, and maybe even a rolling six-month comparison. If you have seasonality, compare it to the same period for the prior year, and if you don't, simply compare it to the prior period.

The more time you spend analyzing how the ratio changes and why, the more clarity you will gain and the more you will learn about how to make decisions that are more financially effective. For example, if this company has established that to have a good financial year, they need to maintain a 3/1 ratio of GP\$/FBP\$, then it can begin to look at the work they are bidding on and challenge their pricing strategy. Perhaps some work they are bidding, given the pricing and the time they will have to spend, is only projected to produce a 2.5/1 ratio. That means if they win that work, it will cannibalize their profitability. If, on the other hand, they can price and win work at 3/1 or 3.2/1, they will be improving their financial performance.

Of course there are many other conditions to consider, but if this firm is doing architectural work for a mix of data centers, multifamily housing, custom homes, tenant improvements, and municipal buildings, then they will have the ability to analyze each category to see how the categories stack up against each other. They might find that while data centers are not as fun and sexy as custom homes, the ratio of Gross Profit to human capital investment is much better with data centers than custom homes. For example, if they found that they could consistently generate a 4/1 ratio on data centers and were only generating 2/1 on custom homes due to the fact that each one is entirely unique, they might decide to wind down their focus on custom homes and go more aggressively into data centers, or at least adjust the ratio between the two.

If you want to build a fabulous economic engine, you have to spend time understanding what is at its core. Then you have to do the analysis and make the necessary adjustments to optimize your financial strategy and outcomes.

Where are your constraints? If you think through each of them, do you gain any clarity on which one of them, if you consistently grew the ratio of profit per that constraint, would allow you to build a fabulous economic engine? This is hard work and takes intentional focus, but the results are absolutely worth the effort.

Cash Conversion Cycles: Don't Grow Broke

Everyone knows that starting a business requires cash, and growing a business requires even more. Growing businesses can consume massive amounts of cash for working capital, facilities, equipment, and operating expenses. Few people understand that *a profitable company that tries to grow too fast can run out of cash*. A key challenge for the leadership team of any growing business is to find the proper balance between consuming cash and generating it. Fail to strike that balance, and even a thriving company can soon find itself out of business…a victim of its own success.

Figure 7.2

The keys to improving your Cash Conversion Cycle are based on making consistent, incremental improvements in the key components impacting the time it takes a dollar invested into the business to return to the business as a dollar received. Referencing the image above, the key components of a Cash Conversion Cycle (CCC) are typically:

Sales Cycle

From the time you start investing in the sales process with a prospect until you have a confirmed order to hand off to operations, you have cash going out of the business. For example, you may have a salesperson take a prospect out to dinner. Cash left the business to pay for the dinner that contributes to the relationship you expect will lead to a confirmed order. Maybe that dinner was a "warm meeting" to ask for a demo or discovery meeting with a broader team. The speed with which your salesperson is able to get the prospect to move from the warm meeting phase to the demo phase can have a positive or negative impact on your CCC.

When the prospect comes for the demo, do you have a clear ask at the end, or is it open ended? Are you intentionally doing everything you can to guide the prospect to make a decision? That decision may be a hard "no," in which case you can stop spending cash to try to convert them and go focus on the next prospect. It may be a "yes," in which case you can quickly move to the next phase. If you allow them to flap endlessly in the wind without getting to a decision, the cash you have invested to this point is also flapping endlessly in the wind, far from your grasp.

Be smart and intentional about decreasing the time it takes for a prospect to move through your sales cycle and you will increase the velocity of cash flowing back into the business.

Production/Inventory/Delivery Cycle

For a business that produces any kind of goods, you can look at your Production and Inventory Cycle as the time from when you procure your inputs to the time they go into Work in Process, then into Finished Goods Inventory, and finally out the door to a customer. Most businesses can find opportunities to improve one or more of these segments within a Production, Inventory, and Delivery Cycle.

For a professional services business, there are still elements of this that apply. While you may not have raw materials and Finished Goods Inventory, an accounting firm still has a Production and Delivery Cycle. The key to improvement is in looking for all the small, incremental improvements you can make in your processes and workflows that will reduce the time it takes to move through the cycle.

Billing and Payment Cycle

This is the amount of time it takes from the delivery of a good or service, to the time the cash lands back in your account. This is a key area where many businesses lose focus and as a result waste cash.

Let's start with the billing cycle. When we dig into the Cash Conversion Cycle with clients, one of the questions we ask is, *"On average, how long does it take from the delivery of your service until the customer receives an invoice?"* We find this is typically much worse with service-based businesses than with product-based businesses. We've literally had clients tell us that they're really busy and it usually takes a week or two to get the invoices out, or worse, that they hold all invoicing until the end of the month. If you take a six-million-dollar business with consistent sales, we could presume that they bill $500,000 monthly, or roughly $125,000 per week. If they take two weeks just to get an invoice to the customer, they are missing an opportunity to add $250,000 of cash to their business because their customers will get their invoices two weeks faster, and assuming the time they pay is relative to the time at which they received and entered the invoice into their system, as is usually the case, the money will come back faster.

In the example above, if the reason it takes two weeks is that the accounting team is understaffed, and they then say that they cannot "justify" adding another person to overhead, that tells us they are driving with blinders on. If adding one administrative person to the finance team would allow them to get invoices out within one business day, then once those invoices cycle through AR, the company's cash will increase by $250,000. For a position that might cost $50,000, which is a fully burdened monthly cost to the company of only around $5,500, justification of the position should not be the issue—the new employee is essentially free. And if within three months of their onboarding, the company has gained a $250,000 improvement in cash, and their three-month investment in the person has been about $15,000, I would argue that is an outstanding Return on Investment and that the additional cash can now be deployed to help them grow the business, which will bring in more profit.

That brings up the next part of this final cycle—the payment cycle. At Erath Veneer, our typical payment terms were Net 30 Days. In reality, customers often tend to pay when they pay, and most organizations simply accept it as they don't want to upset a customer. We were no different. Before we started really focusing on it, our average days to pay, with terms of Net 30 Days, was running in the mid-fifty-day range, and our Accounts Receivable (AR) would vary around $2,500,000.

There was a time when we would have a member of our accounting team call customers who were past due to inquire about payment. The problem was that most of those calls would be routed to someone within our customer's accounting team, which resulted in the two people on the phone having misaligned objectives. Our collections team member was trying to get cash in as quickly as possible, and the person they were talking to was trying to hold on to cash as long as they could. When we made the change to task our salespeople with collecting their own AR, they would talk with their colleague, the buyer, on the other side of the open invoice, and there was always a better relationship between those two people. Also, the buyer often had more leverage within their own company, as one of their main objectives was to maintain vendor relationships to ensure they had access to the resources they needed, so there was an incentive to collaborate.

A few other things we did that had a measurable impact included modifying how we expressed the payment terms. In addition to stating "Net 30 Days" on the invoice, we would also list the date that marked the thirty days, so instead of just reading "Net 30 Days," our invoices would read, "Net 30 Days—Due February 3." There is always an assumption from the seller that Net 30 Days means from the date of the invoice, but the buyer almost always takes the position that it is from the date the invoice was received. By including the actual due date, in many instances, that alone improved the average days it took a specific customer to pay by three to five days.

Think about that…if one of our customers typically carried $100,000 in AR and their average days to pay was fifty, and just the minor modification above led to a small change in behavior on their end that got us paid just three days faster, that is a 6 percent reduction in AR days for that client, which is worth $100,000 × 6% = $6,000 of improved cash flow. Multiply that across multiple accounts, and the numbers add up very quickly.

Another thing we did was to start sending a "friendly reminder" of an upcoming due date. Many companies wait until an invoice goes past due to begin communicating about that particular invoice, and I believe that is a missed opportunity. We implemented a simple process by which we would send a friendly reminder ten days before an invoice was due, with a very positive short note about how much we valued the relationship and appreciated their collaboration and timely payment. If we knew who within their accounting team held the keys to getting us paid, we would send the note to them, and we would always copy the buyer. It was a soft, subtle reminder that they needed good vendors, and we needed good customers who would live up to their obligations to pay us on time.

Just implementing those two simple and essentially zero-cost adjustments, our average AR days dropped from the mid-fifties to the upper forties. While that may not sound like a big move, the impact of a seven-day average reduction in AR days was an improvement of about 13 percent, and with an average AR of around $2,500,000, a 13 percent improvement created a roughly $325,000 improvement in our cash position that we could more rapidly redeploy back into growing the business.

Cash and Cash Flow Forecasting

Most entrepreneurs are familiar with the statement, "Revenue is vanity, profit is sanity, and cash is king." While this statement is not untrue, I think there is a significant flaw…I would agree with those who say it is not "cash" that is king but "cash flow."

The reason to consider cash flow more important than cash is due to its dynamic nature and its direct reflection of a company's operational health. This is also why reviewing not only your Profit and Loss statement monthly but also your balance sheet, and especially your Cash Flow Statement, is imperative. Here are several reasons why this is so impactful:

- **Timeliness and Relevance:** Cash flow reflects the inflow and outflow of cash over a specific period, providing a real-time view of a company's financial situation. It accounts for operational expenses, investments, and financing activities, offering a more accurate and current assessment compared to a snapshot of cash at a single point in time.
- **Operational Sustainability:** Positive cash flow indicates that a company is generating more cash than it is spending, signifying the ability to cover its ongoing expenses, invest in growth opportunities, and meet its financial obligations. It ensures that the day-to-day operations can continue smoothly.
- **Investment and Growth:** Cash flow is crucial for funding expansion, innovation, and strategic initiatives. Companies with healthy cash flows have the ability to invest in research, development, acquisitions, or new market penetration, driving growth and competitiveness.
- **Debt Servicing and Financial Health:** Cash flow is instrumental in servicing debt obligations, including interest payments and debt reduction. Lenders often assess cash flow to determine a company's ability to repay loans. A strong cash flow history can improve creditworthiness and reduce borrowing costs.
- **Risk Management:** Regular monitoring of cash flow helps identify potential financial issues or liquidity problems in advance. It allows management to make informed decisions to mitigate risks, adjust strategies, or seek additional financing if necessary.
- **Investor and Stakeholder Confidence:** Investors and stakeholders often scrutinize cash flow statements to assess a company's financial stability and growth potential. A consistent positive cash flow demonstrates financial discipline and can attract investment and confidence from stakeholders.

While cash reserves are essential for short-term liquidity and emergencies, maintaining a healthy flow of cash is critical for the sustained success, growth, and stability of a business. Organizations with strong cash flow management are better positioned to navigate economic downturns, seize opportunities, and thrive in the long run.

Cash on Hand

There is an important need to balance, in every organization's particular circumstance, how you approach cash on hand, and you need to understand your cash flow forecasting to strike that balance. I'll use a specific example from my own business, Next Level Growth, to help illustrate this.

In the early days of Next Level Growth, I was a solopreneur as I left the world of manufacturing and transitioned to coaching. My operating expenses and overheads were low, and the business generated very good cash flow. I had an outstanding but relatively small facility with a monthly lease just under $4,000 and not many other fixed expenses. I kept at least $10,000 of cash on hand in case we had a downturn, but otherwise, I could shut off variable expenses quickly, and the delta between monthly cash flow and fixed costs was high, so there was not much for me to be concerned about.

As I began to build out a firm of business guides, relocated to a new, much larger and more expensive office, and built out significantly more resources and collateral, things changed. I started spending money on graphic design, marketing, public relations, additional team members to support our growing business, and a host of other investments and subscriptions that needed to be made in order to support a growing business.

When thinking about how much cash on hand I needed to maintain as a buffer for slow times, I needed to get a clear picture of what my total monthly cost structure was. What was a fully fixed cost? What costs were entirely variable? What costs were in between the two extremes? In my case, as of the writing of this book, I have roughly $80,000 in average total monthly expenses required to run our firm, of which about $30,000 are fixed, and about half of the remaining expenses would negatively impact the business if we had to cut them out.

Some organizations look at cash on hand through the lens of, "If our revenue dropped to zero, how much do we want to have in reserves to survive?" Different leaders have different levels of risk tolerance, and that reality needs to play into the way this is approached. If you have a very low tolerance for risk, this is likely the right approach to give you peace of mind. If, on the other hand, you are highly risk-tolerant, this will probably cause you to tie up too much cash, cash that you would rather be redeploying in growth opportunities.

The balance I try to strike is to look at scenarios where we have a drop in revenue of 25 percent and 50 percent. When the pandemic hit in 2020, we had an almost immediate drop in revenue of about 30 percent and it lasted for around five months. When I consider my business model, we could quickly shut off about $25,000 of the $80,000 monthly spend without having a meaningful negative impact on the quality of how the business operates. These are variable expenses that are nice to afford and do allow us to enhance the way we do things, but they are not necessary for survival. Since I have about $25,000 that is discretionary, that brings my "downturn" monthly nut to about $55,000, and my "survival mode" to around $30,000.

To be able to operate in an environment where revenues and net cash flow from operations drop 25 percent, if we carry $60,000 cash on hand, together with cash that is still flowing but at a reduced rate, we can go at least six months without having to make more drastic moves.

In our particular circumstance, if we carry less than that, we're putting our business at risk in a sudden downturn, and if we carry more, we're tying up cash that could be reinvested in growing the business. As the founder, for my level of risk tolerance and desire for growth, that is a balance I'm comfortable with.

Cash Flow Forecasting and Staying Ahead of the Curve

Depending on the business model, there are varying degrees of accuracy in ninety-day cash flow forecasting. When we ask the finance team leader of a client company if they maintain a cash flow forecast, we sometimes get pushback that, "Our cash flow is too unpredictable to forecast," or, "There are too many variables for it to be accurate and valuable." This is usually code for either "I'm not sure how to do it" or "I don't have time to do the work required."

Either way, if the leader of your finance team is not providing some sort of a meaningful cash flow forecast and reviewing it with key executives frequently, I would encourage you to insist that they do, as that is a significant part of their job and responsibility to the organization. Regardless of the variabilities that exist in any given industry, based on historical trends, seasonality, and sufficient data, I believe every business can and should maintain a detailed cash flow forecast with as much accuracy and as close to ninety days out as their specific business model allows.

If you disagree, go back to the section in Chapter 3 on the Next Level Accountability Chart and Most Critical Outcome. I believe the leader of the finance team has a fiduciary responsibility to protect the financial health and cash flow of the business. If they are not forecasting cash and reporting to the team on a regular basis, they cannot fulfill their responsibility to protect cash flow.

At Next Level Growth, our cash flows into and out of five different accounts and is based on a methodology I learned from reading the book *Profit First* by Mike Michalowicz. Two are for receiving payments, one is for paying operating expenses, and two are for savings—one for safety-net cash on hand and one for building cash for quarterly taxes, which, since we are an S-Corporation, I have to pay through my personal tax return and quarterly estimated tax payments.

Our controller maintains a spreadsheet that pulls from various resources and includes some manual adjustments. It shows me the ninety-day forecast for cash flow in and out of each account, together with an aggregate column that shows me total forecasted cash looking ninety days out. We have lots of variables, too. If we spend more or less than expected on marketing in a given month, the forecast has to be adjusted. If we add a client or lose a client, the forecast has to adjust. But knowing what to expect as we predict the next ninety days of cash allows me to see trends and concerns coming long before they arrive…and that helps us make better, more timely decisions and adjustments.

> Leading a business without clear and updated cash flow forecasts would be like a pilot leaving on a cross-country trip without checking the weather forecasts along the route or at the destination and without some of their key navigational equipment functioning. I wouldn't want to be a passenger on that plane.

The Power of Incremental Change

"Small hinges swing big doors."[30]

—widely attributed to W. Clement Stone

The last discipline of *Growing Profits and Cash Flow* that I want to address is what we call *The Power of Incremental Change*. When it comes to a focus on financial improvements, many teams either don't know where to start or they let themselves believe they are too busy to do the work. As a result, their profit and cash flow are a by-product that just happens to them, not something they intentionally go after and achieve.

The idea behind The Power of Incremental Change is to think about everything within your influence that affects things like your Profit per X and your Cash Conversion Cycle. Take each of them one at a time, and instead of focusing on coming up with some big initiative, think about what it would look like to improve it by 1 percent or one day. Here are a few examples:

One of our clients is a distributor and supplier of parts for home services contractors. When their Guide looked into their pricing strategy, they found that almost all of their products were priced on a very basic markup equation, using different factors based on the product type. It had been years since they had done any secret shopping to really understand what their competitors' pricing was, and they were not doing any market price testing. With more than ten branches across two states, their Guide sensed that there was a big opportunity.

They decided to take one of their branches and run a test. Based on demand, and just focusing on parts, not full equipment systems, they implemented small price increases of 1 to 5 percent on all of the shelf

---

30 "Big Doors Swing on Little Hinges," Stan Phelps Speaks, accessed December 5, 2024, https://stanphelps.com/big-doors-swing-on-little-hinges-w-clement-stone/.

items, with an overall average of roughly a 3 percent increase across all parts sold in the store. These were the items that a contractor would buy when they walked into the branch. They held these prices for a month, checking the beta-test branch sales to the other stores' sales on a daily and weekly basis to see if there was any drop in volume. What they found was very eye-opening.

Their Guide had shared a Next Level Growth document with them called *Price Increases, Discounts and Impact on Gross Profit Dollars* (see Figures 7.3 and 7.4), which breaks down, based on your Gross Margin, how much volume you can lose relative to any percentage price increase without losing any actual dollars of Gross Profit. In the case of these parts, the company averaged around 50 percent Gross Profit before the price increases.

At that Gross Margin, with a 3 percent price increase, they could have experienced a drop in volume of up to 5.6 percent without losing any actual Gross Profit dollars. The reality, after an entire month, was that their volume remained unchanged relative to their control group of stores, which means they generated significantly more Gross Profit dollars without spending any additional dollars of operating expenses. As a result, all of the gain fell to the bottom line.

From there, they started implementing the same strategy across all of their branches and did market testing to see what price levels the market would bear. Just six months later, they were anticipating the adjustment to their pricing strategy, and these small incremental changes would add more than $300,000 of annual net profit and additional cash flow.

Another one of our clients is an auto dealership with multiple locations selling used cars. Their Profit per X is *Net Profit per Unit Sold*, so that is the key to their economic engine. Given the high-interest-rate environment and credit tightening of 2023 and 2024, driving price was an uphill battle, so their Guide started by focusing on cost and profit only and asked them to make a list of all the costs they could control or influence that impacted Profit per Unit Sold. This is an exercise we call the *Million Dollar Whiteboard* because we often find at least one million dollars of incremental value over a period of just a few short years or less, depending on the size of the business. A few of the many items on that list were:

- Reconditioning Cost
- Advertising Expense
- Acquisition Cost
- Transportation Cost

Taking them one by one, they discussed the option to start doing some of their reconditioning in-house instead of outsourcing all of it as they had been doing. By bringing all of their reconditioning in-house, they estimated that they would be able to save around $100 per unit when considering the additional cost it would take them to expand their recon department combined with the savings of not having to pay an outside vendor for the vehicles they brought in-house.

They decided to work on improvements to their referral strategy and "self-generated traffic" strategy with their sales team to create more "free" leads and estimated they could reduce their advertising cost per unit by $50.

By making a few adjustments to their buying strategy to increase the percentage of street buys relative to auction buys, they felt that the savings in auction fees alone by adjusting the ratios would save them $25 per unit.

As a by-product of the buying strategy adjustments and a decision to renegotiate their transportation contracts, they believed they could reduce their transportation per unit by another $25.

In all, they expected the above changes would result in a savings of $200 per unit. With three locations and average annual unit sales of 3,500 vehicles, they anticipated just these four changes alone would increase their net profits by $700,000, and if they could keep those gained efficiencies as their unit sales grew over time, that savings would grow with them year over year. The long-term impact of just that one exercise can yield millions of dollars of added profit and cash flow over a period of just a few years.

Price Strategy—Increases Versus Discounts

Very few organizations I meet really focus on their pricing strategy and, in fact, most of them are quick to discount prices and rarely consider the power of raising prices. As I pointed out in the story about the distributor, I believe organizations should be just as intentional about their pricing strategy as they are on expense management.

I'll share two brief, and powerful, points on this. Think about your favorite restaurant. Let's just say that the average ticket value for the restaurant is $50 per person. Most companies are afraid to raise prices because they are concerned they will lose too many customers, and restaurants are no different.

But consider if, as a guest of the restaurant, they adjusted their prices across the menu by just 1 to 3 percent, so that the average ticket value went from $50 to $51 per person. I cannot imagine there would be any drop-off in traffic or frequency as a result of such a small change. However, if the restaurant has twenty locations, and they average one hundred guests per evening per location, that's $2,000 per evening. If they are open six nights per week that's $12,000 per week, times fifty-two weeks, is $624,000 over the course of a year.

If a business operates on a 50 percent gross margin, it could raise prices by 2 percent and afford to lose nearly 4 percent in volume and still generate the same dollars of Gross Profit. If their gross margin was 30 percent, they could afford to lose up to 6.25 percent of their volume and still generate the same dollars of Gross Profit.

Gross Margin

	20%	30%	40%	50%	60%
2%	9.09%	6.25%	4.76%	3.85%	3.23%
3%	13.04%	9.09%	6.98%	5.66%	4.76%
4%	16.67%	11.76%	9.09%	7.41%	6.25%
5%	20.00%	14.29%	11.11%	9.09%	7.89%
10%	33.33%	25.00%	20.00%	16.67%	14.29%
15%	42.86%	33.33%	27.27%	23.08%	20.00%
20%	50.00%	40.00%	33.33%	28.57%	25.00%
25%	55.56%	45.45%	38.46%	33.33%	29.41%
30%	60.00%	50.00%	42.86%	37.50%	33.33%

Price Increase

Figure 7.3
Download this form and more at FiveObsessions.com

Another point I want you to consider is the negative real impact on Gross Profit dollars of discounting your prices. Typically, discounts happen in the range of 10 percent or more. For this example, take the same company operating at a gross margin of 50 percent. If they decided to discount their prices by 10 percent to attract more sales, they would need to see an increase in sales of 25 percent just to generate the same dollars of Gross Profit. If their gross margin was only 30 percent, they would need to see sales increase by 50 percent just to keep the same actual dollars of Gross Profit flowing into the business with a 10 percent discount on price. Good luck with that!

Gross Margin

Price Discount	20%	30%	40%	50%	60%
-2%	11.11%	7.14%	5.26%	4.17%	3.45%
-3%	17.65%	11.11%	8.11%	6.38%	5.26%
-4%	25.00%	15.38%	11.11%	8.70%	7.14%
-5%	33.33%	20.00%	14.29%	11.11%	9.09%
-10%	100.00%	50.00%	33.33%	25.00%	20.00%
-15%	300.00%	100.00%	60.00%	42.86%	33.33%
-20%	Not Possible	200.00%	100.00%	66.67%	50.00%
-25%	Not Possible	500.00%	166.67%	100.00%	71.43%
-30%	Not Possible	Not Possible	300.00%	150.00%	100.00%

Figure 7.4

Download this form and more at FiveObsessions.com

YOU MUST DO THE WORK
TO GET THE RESULTS

These disciplines around growing profit and cash flow, if you will begin to focus on them and prioritize them, will yield outstanding results over time, and they will yield results that will remain with you for the life of your business. On average, companies working with a Next Level Growth Partner and Business Guide grow their estimated Enterprise Value by a factor of 5.9 times over their first five years, and we've had several clients who desired an exit achieve actual results equating to real growth in value of ten to twenty-five times in as little as four to six years. As I said earlier, *effort is your responsibility.*

For help exploring the many ways you can excel at *Growing Profits and Cash Flow*, consider working with my clone at **AskMichaelErath.com**.

We have a quote from author Larry Winget on the wall in one of our hallways at Next Level Growth, which I shared at the beginning of this book. *"The only thing standing between you and what you want, is you and what you are not willing to do."*[31] Intentionally *Growing Profits and Cash Flow* is hard work because it requires you to spend time working on your business, not in it.

These are the *Five Obsessions of Elite Organizations*. To succeed, you must be disciplined and focused, and you must be willing to do the

---

31 Larry Winget, *What's Wrong with Damn Near Everything! How the Collapse of Core Values Is Destroying Us and How to Fix It* (Wiley, 2017).

work. For those who are willing, the rewards are great, but there is one final component to building an elite and enduring organization and I will explore it with you in the next chapter, "Emotionally Intelligent Leadership and Building Elite Organizations."

Chapter 8

EMOTIONALLY INTELLIGENT LEADERSHIP AND BUILDING ELITE ORGANIZATIONS

"When dealing with people, remember
you are not dealing with creatures of logic,
but with creatures of emotion."

—DALE CARNEGIE

There is one final and very critical factor you must commit to if you are going to truly succeed in utilizing the Five Obsessions framework and build an elite organization. You have to hire, develop, and retain leaders at every level of the organization who truly understand and display the soft skills necessary to build relationships with team members. These are leaders who will work collaboratively both across the various departments within the organization and also up and down the chain of command. If you don't focus on this, and if you hire or elevate people into leadership roles who do not have these soft skills and the ability to build relationships, you will never have an environment where people will bring their very best to their work. One important concept we teach our clients to help with this is the SCARF® Model from Dr. David Rock, director of the NeuroLeadership Institute.[32]

I DON'T GIVE TENS

I cannot tell you how many times in the years we've spent as Business Guides we've heard leaders, when asked to rate someone or something on a one to ten scale, say, "I don't give tens."

Whenever we hear that, we like to follow the statement with a question that always has the same answer, "Why don't you give tens?" So far, 100 percent of the time, the answer is either "People can always do better," or "If I rate their performance ten out of ten, they'll stop pushing themselves."

While that answer may be understandable, it is also highly debatable. If a basketball player goes eight for eight from the free-throw line, could they have done better? Of course not. Would you expect them to stop trying as hard in the next game? I doubt it. But we get it. The premise behind the philosophy is based on the fear that if a leader gives a team member a ten out of ten, even when they deserve it, that team member will slack off and stop trying to improve.

Sadly, that mindset assumes the worst of people, and it also shows a lack of understanding of how the limbic system works in the human brain.

32 Mind Tools Content Team, "David Rock's SCARF Model," Mind Tools, accessed December 5, 2024, https://www.mindtools.com/akswgc0/david-rocks-scarf-model.

THE UNINTENDED CONSEQUENCE OF
A "THEY CAN ALWAYS DO BETTER" MINDSET

We typically follow this response by asking the leader if they think that over time, always telling people they could do better, even when those people exceed expectations, might eventually cause them to give up and stop trying so hard because they may begin to feel like their best is never going to be good enough. The leader almost always agrees that this is a likely long-term result.

Every once in a while, we encounter a leader who refuses to consider an alternative approach and insists on being overly tough on everyone, as if they believe they can just grind performance out of their team. In every single case we have observed, and we never know if it will happen in weeks or if it will take as much as a year or more, that leader eventually leaves the organization. Sometimes, they leave on their own because it becomes increasingly evident over time, as other leaders grow to embrace a more productive approach to building an elite organization, that they are just not a good fit. Other times, they're asked to leave because the owner eventually sees the collateral damage being done by their leadership style and finally takes action.

THE SCIENCE BEHIND APPRECIATION
AND THE LIMBIC SYSTEM

When people are constantly being ground on to do better by a tough boss, their amygdala starts to send signals to the brain that trigger a fight-or-flight response. As a result, neurochemicals like adrenaline and cortisol are released into the bloodstream. Depending on the extremity of the situation, this can actually cause the prefrontal cortex, the part of the brain that controls our cognitive abilities, to begin to shut down. When the prefrontal cortex begins to shut down, it becomes harder on those affected to think clearly and make good decisions, which is the exact opposite of what their leader usually intends.

Conversely, when team members feel appreciated and have a healthy relationship with the leaders to whom they report, the opposite happens. Different neurochemicals, like oxytocin, serotonin, and dopamine, are released. This will often cause the team members to feel a sense of belonging and engagement, which enhances their commitment to the team and leader and often their performance as well.

In a 2021 article, "'Great Attrition' or 'Great Attraction'? The Choice is Yours," published by McKinsey & Co. in the *McKinsey Quarterly*, researchers surveyed 5,774 employees of working age across multiple industries and five countries (Australia, Canada, Singapore, the United Kingdom, and the United States). They also surveyed 250 managers specializing in talent (such as chief talent officers). These managers were evenly split between large organizations with more than $1 billion in revenues, and midsize ones, with revenues from fifty million to one billion dollars.[33]

Employers and employees were given a list of twenty-three reasons people leave their jobs and asked to answer one question to help the researchers understand both why employees were leaving and why employers thought their employees were leaving. Employees were asked: To what extent did the following factors impact your decision to leave your last job? The possible answers were *not at all, slightly, moderately, very much,* and *extremely*. Employers were asked: Why do you think employees are choosing to leave your organization now? They were asked to select all that apply.

---

33 Aaron De Smet et al., "'Great Attrition' or 'Great Attraction'? The Choice Is Yours," *McKinsey Quarterly,* September 8, 2021, https://www.mckinsey.com/capabilities/people-and-organizational-performance/our-insights/great-attrition-or-great-attraction-the-choice-is-yours.

According to employers, they thought that the most common reasons employees were leaving had to do with either inadequate compensation or looking for a better job. When that is what you think, you come up with proposals like retention bonuses or other ways to throw more money at them to get them to stay, which is exactly what was happening in 2021 and 2022.

What was fascinating about the results was how the employees actually answered the survey. The top three reasons they were leaving were that they did not feel valued by the organization, they did not feel valued by their manager, and they did not feel a sense of belonging.

Employers and employees were completely misaligned, and the resulting attrition that occurred came to be known as the *Great Resignation*. The irony is that exactly what it would have taken to keep employees from leaving would have cost the organizations absolutely nothing. To understand this better, it is important to understand how the limbic brain works.

THE SCARF MODEL

Dr. David Rock has done extensive work on this subject and has created what he calls the SCARF Model. This model explains how, as leaders, our behaviors, and the way we interact with our teams, can cause our team members' brains to respond to five key social needs in ways that are largely beyond their control. It explains how the results of our interactions and leadership style can have a significant, often unintended impact on our team members' engagement and performance.

In a nutshell, SCARF is an acronym for: *Status, Certainty, Autonomy, Relatedness, and Fairness*. These are five social needs of humans that a leader can affect through their words and actions in ways that cause nearly uncontrollable chemical reactions in the brain and ultimately impact the effectiveness of the people around them. At a very high level, you just need to understand that when any of us are in an environment where we experience a threat response, chemicals are released that affect our brains in ways that make it harder to think clearly. Our brains work in this way to protect us...to make us want to move away from the threat. Conversely, when we are in an environment where we feel rewarded or appreciated, we experience a reward response. The reward response activates different chemicals in our brains and creates a desire to move toward or engage more closely with whatever caused us to experience the reward response.

SCARF EXPLAINED

The following is a brief summary of each component of the SCARF Model. For more on this, please see Dr. Rock's book, *Your Brain at Work*.

The key thing to remember as a leader is that if your leadership style and disposition are consistently creating threat responses in your team members, you are likely undermining their ability to perform at a high level without even realizing it. You are actually working against your objectives. On the other hand, if you are intentional about balancing correction where needed with affirming and appreciating the positive things your team members are doing, you will get all of the benefits resulting from the reward response. Of course, there are times where you have to be firm and direct, but it is important to always do so within the context of the SCARF Model. The more you focus on balancing correction and coaching with appreciation, the more trust you will build with others, which makes difficult conversations easier and more effective when they do have to happen.

Status

If a leader berates an employee, especially in public, that action diminishes the team member's status and can make them feel attacked or cause them to think less of themselves, which creates a threat response. The employee's amygdala starts to fire, and adrenaline is released into the bloodstream. That is why most of us, when under attack, experience sweaty palms and shaky voices. We cannot always think clearly in the moment. Sometimes, we get angry and fight back, arguing with or yelling back at our boss or others. Either way, the neurochemicals in our brain make it difficult, if not impossible, for us to think clearly and rationally in the moment. Further, these adrenaline releases lead to a buildup of cortisol in our bloodstream, which has longer-term negative effects on us. It actually makes it more difficult to think clearly, which then makes it difficult to focus on our performance.

When a leader shows appreciation for positive performance or behaviors, team members will experience a sense of elevated status which will lead to a reward response. Dopamine, serotonin, and oxytocin are released, and that makes us feel good, even somewhat euphoric. As humans, we want more of that feeling, and more often than not, we will adjust behaviors and actions to do more of the things that led to the appreciation and created the reward response.

Certainty

If a leader creates an environment of uncertainty, like constantly making people feel that their job is on the line and they could be terminated at any moment, it creates a threat response. The fear team members are constantly facing negatively impacts their performance because the constant fight-or-flight mode reduces the functionality of their prefrontal cortex. If, on the other hand, leaders establish clear expectations, coach team members where they need it, and help those team members feel that the leader has their backs and is supportive, they will have a sense of certainty, of security, and experience a reward response.

An example of this came during the pandemic of 2020. Many businesses faced very difficult times, and people throughout organizations became very fearful due to the uncertainty of what the future would hold and whether they would be able to keep their jobs and provide for themselves and their families. During that time, we coached our clients to hold frequent "all-hands" meetings or send out frequent communications, updating team members on the current state of the business, the current issues leadership was focusing on, and what they were expecting over the next one to four weeks.

By shifting focus from the typical quarterly and annual all-hands meeting rhythms to just focusing on one week or one month at a time, people felt more in control and more certain, which calmed the fear. When facing a crisis, it is often helpful to focus on shorter spans of time and set clear and attainable short-term goals and tasks to keep your focus on more controllable things.

Autonomy

When a leader is constantly micromanaging a team member, that team member will often lose any sense of autonomy in their role, and the result is a threat response. Nobody likes to be micromanaged, and it is often something we perceive as a threat. Conversely, when a leader, again with clearly communicated expectations, allows team members the freedom to make decisions on their own and have a reasonable degree of autonomy in their roles, that sense of autonomy causes them to experience a reward response.

Think about the last time you were micromanaged. How did that make you feel? Did it help you work better and make fewer mistakes?

Likely not. The pressure of being micromanaged causes us to work in a constant state of elevated stress and anxiety, and nobody can be at their best for very long under those circumstances.

Relatedness

Human beings are small-group animals. Most people do not like being in large crowds for extended periods of time and also don't like extended periods of isolation. We are tribal creatures. When the environment at work pits people against one another in order to drive performance, or even when we fail to focus on building a culture that connects people to one another, they often feel isolated and alone at work. That results in a threat response.

When people work in an environment with others who share common values and work together as a healthy team, even though most of us have some level of a competitive spirit, the clear common goals, under the guidance of healthy leadership, allow people to experience a reward response. It provides a sense of belonging, as though we have found our tribe.

Fairness

Lastly, when team members experience a lack of fairness, whether they are the target or they observe someone else being treated unfairly, they will almost always experience a threat response. Think about experiences in your own lifetime when you have witnessed unfairness or been subject to it. If you can put yourself back in that moment, it is likely you will recognize that you experienced the same signs and symptoms of a threat response.

Conversely, when people feel that they work in an environment where they know people are treated fairly, they experience a reward response, especially in challenging situations where fairness is tested. In the end, even when hard decisions have to be made, like terminating a relationship with a long-term employee, if people sense that things were handled in a fair way, they are much more open and understanding, and you avoid the negative consequences of a threat response.

I would strongly encourage you to teach the SCARF Model to all of your leaders, managers, and supervisors. It is one of the many basic soft skills that we believe everyone given the responsibility of leadership should learn and embrace.

A PERSONAL STORY OF AN ORGANIZATION THAT GETS IT RIGHT

Oftentimes, when we first mention the concept of an elite organization, especially around a *Culture of Performance*, people initially think about a hard-driving culture that is tough on team members. They think of organizations that follow the Jack Welch style at General Electric during his tenure as CEO, where he famously fired the bottom 10 percent of the workforce every year. In our belief, that kind of fear-based performance culture not only isn't necessary, but it also rarely works in the long run, as evidenced by the rise and eventual fall of General Electric.

In November of 2023, our youngest son, Zachary, started working at the Fairmont Scottsdale Princess Resort as a temporary employee during their *Christmas at the Princess* event. He had just turned twenty-four years old. When the event concluded, he was brought over as a full-time employee and began working as an experience concierge in the resort's exclusive Privado Villas division.

If you've experienced the Fairmont brand, and if you've been fortunate to have experienced the Scottsdale Princess, you will know that the brand has a very high standard for guest experience. In order to protect and consistently provide that, they have a very high bar when it comes to the behaviors and performance of their team members. What has been so refreshing to see is the way they build a high-performing culture through a balance of intentional signs of appreciation and personal connection with their team members.

If you are a parent of adult children, you will understand me when I say that when your adult children work for a bad boss, you get to hear all of the complaints and horror stories. My wife and I have heard plenty of those over the years that we've had adult children. On the other hand, when you hear your adult children constantly talking about how wonderful their managers and bosses are and how appreciated they feel not only by those they directly report to but also by the organization as a whole, you feel peace knowing that they are in a good place to grow and develop.

David Miller is the hotel manager at the Fairmont Scottsdale Princess, and Jack Miller (no relation to David) is the regional vice president. While Zachary is far removed from them in the organizational structure, every time either of them sees him on the property, they go out of their way to say hello and be friendly to him. And it's not just him, it's everyone. At a 2024 training meeting in advance of opening their new Privado Welcome Center, David Miller noticed that he and Zachary were wearing nearly identical sports coats, so he grabbed Zachary and had one of their colleagues take a photo, which Zachary's manager, Amanda Isbell, later posted on her LinkedIn account.

Figure 8.1
L to R: Our son, Zachary Erath, with David Miller,
Hotel Manager, Fairmont Scottsdale Princess Resort

For a young team member who is just getting started on a career path in hospitality, small but intentional gestures to connect on a human level like this are incredibly powerful in drawing them closer to the organization, which creates significantly better engagement and ultimately, performance. In that moment, David's actions caused Zachary to feel as though his status was elevated. It also created an enhanced feeling of relatedness toward a leader who is several layers removed from Zachary's position. Both of those things created a reward response and triggered a chain reaction of positive neurochemical reactions in Zachary's brain that he could not control, but the results of which you can clearly see in the smile on his face.

Over a recent dinner, Zachary was talking with his mother and me about work and shared with us that he has never worked in an organization where the team of leaders he reports to are as helpful and supportive as at the Fairmont. Throughout his onboarding and training, while he was being corrected when he would make a mistake or not remember a step, it was always balanced with recognition and appreciation when he did things well. The team he reports to has very high standards and coaches him where he needs to learn and grow. At the same time, they make sure he is very clear on what is expected of him and that he feels their appreciation when he does things well. This leads to a more trusting relationship. One where it feels safe to receive critical feedback, where he has certainty in where he stands with his managers, and where he knows that they support him and want to see him grow in his career.

As a result, an emotional connection has been built with his coworkers, his management team, and the brand as a whole. That emotional connection results in him feeling like he never wants to let down or disappoint the people he works with and works for. The by-product of that is an even stronger desire to bring his very best every day, and that kind of attitude is infectious in a very positive way. Everyone on his team shares that same feeling and desire. They helped him get to that place in his first ninety days not by browbeating him and grinding on him but by coaching and mentoring him…by connecting with him. They took time to understand how he learns best and guided him accordingly. He has expressed to us that as his career advances over time, it is his hope that it will always be as part of the Fairmont family.

Going back to the McKinsey study, the team of leaders who Zachary works for have created and maintained an environment where he feels valued by his managers, especially Amanda, who he directly reports to. He feels valued by the organization as a whole, and he feels a sense of belonging and having found his tribe. Those are the key ingredients you must have if you are going to develop and retain your A-Players over the long-term. On our YouTube channel there is a playlist called "Great People." On that playlist you can find a video from Simon Sinek called "Trusting Teams" that does a fantastic job of further explaining the importance of emotionally intelligent leadership in building lasting greatness.

To create what they have at the Fairmont Scottsdale Princess takes intentionality. It takes a team of leaders who are values aligned and focused and who have the emotional intelligence to create a genuine culture where people care about each other. When the team members feel this connected and supported, the guests will be very well cared for. You must invest in finding and developing emotionally intelligent leaders if you are ever going to achieve this in your own organization.

Get all your questions answered about building an organization around emotionally intelligent leadership at **AskMichaelErath.com**.

TAKE YOUR BUSINESS AND YOUR LIFE TO THE NEXT LEVEL

"You are my creator, but I am your master."

—MARY SHELLEY

THE TRAP OF CONTENTMENT

So many entrepreneurial leaders become content with good being good enough and end up trapped in their own businesses. The problem is not unlike what Mary Shelley wrote about in her 1818 novel *Frankenstein*. In the novel, scientist Victor Frankenstein, through an unorthodox scientific experiment, successfully creates life from something that before was lifeless. In many ways, entrepreneurs do the same thing. They create something where there once was nothing.

In the novel, the creation of Victor Frankenstein eventually turns against him and seeks to destroy him. For entrepreneurs, there almost always comes a time when it feels like the business you've created begins to turn against you and, in many ways, feels like it is out to destroy you. For some of you, that may have happened already, as it has for me, and you've moved past that stage. For others, it may be happening now. If you are not currently experiencing that feeling, and if you have not already, statistics show that with very few exceptions, at some point, you will. It's what Cameron Herold, former COO of 1-800-GOT-JUNK? and founder of the COO Alliance, refers to as the "Entrepreneurial Roller Coaster."[34]

As I mentioned earlier, I was fortunate to spend fifteen of the first twenty years of my career as a member of the peer groups YPO and EO, with a short time also spent in Vistage. From my time with each of those organizations, one thing became very clear to me: *Most entrepreneurs, to some degree, achieve success at the expense of their relationships, their time with family, their physical health, or their emotional health.*

I created Next Level Growth, and ultimately decided to write this book, because I believe it doesn't have to be that way.

COHERENCE: HOW 1 + 1 = 4

"Like going to the gym, it is not the intensity of your effort, but the consistency of your effort that leads to success."[35]

—SIMON SINEK

34 Cameron Herold, "Highs and Lows of CEOs: How to Successfully Ride the Entrepreneurial Roller Coaster with Cameron Herold at Joe Polish's Genius Network™," May 2018, in *Genius Network*, podcast, 21:30, https://geniusnetwork.com/podcast/highs-and-lows-of-ceos-how-to-successfully-ride-the -entrepreneurial-roller-coaster-with-cameron-herold-at-joe-polishs-genius-network/.

35 Simon Sinek, "Next Level Growth—Simon Sinek on the Importance of Consistency," Next Level Growth, December 10, 2023, YouTube video, 2:03, https://youtu.be/Pb1KA0-Dy4g?si=nudcYCyLLToexVcp.

In order to achieve true success in building an elite organization and become a category of one in your market, you must reach a point where you are consistently focused on steady improvement of all Five Obsessions. That said, I do believe most organizations will best build momentum by focusing first on *Great People* and *Optimized Playbooks*. That is the first foundation. Ultimately, however, to truly become elite requires you to be excellent in each of the Five Obsessions. When you do this well, you will experience a compounding effect: *coherence*, which Jim Collins discusses in *Good to Great*. In talking about the "flywheel effect," Collins references a conversation he had with physics professor R. J. Peterson. Here is what Collins wrote about the conversation and the concept.

> When I look over the good-to-great transformations, the one word that keeps coming to mind is consistency. Another word offered to me by physics professor R. J. Peterson is coherence. "What is one plus one?" he asked, then paused for effect. "Four! In physics, we have been talking about the idea of coherence, the magnifying effect of one factor upon another. In reading about the flywheel, I couldn't help but think of the principle of coherence." However you phrase it, the basic idea is the same: Each piece of the system reinforces the other parts of the system to form an integrated whole that is much more powerful than the sum of the parts. It is only through consistency over time, through multiple generations, that you get maximum results.[36]

When you start taking your investment in *Great People* seriously, you will find that building the organization around a core of A-Players, people who perform two to four times above the average for their roles and who are aligned with and living your core values, you will get a return far greater than any investment you have to make to recruit and retain them. C-Players don't like working with A-Players, and

---

36 Collins, *Good to Great*, 182.

A-Players don't like working with C-Players. As leaders, it is your job to recruit and retain A-Players while maintaining a robust system for coaching up or coaching out all of your underperformers. You cannot become a category of one with mediocre people.

Steve Jobs is widely attributed as having said, "If you are working on something exciting that you really care about, you don't have to be pushed. The vision pulls you." As you build your organization around a never-ending quest to level up your teams, you have to capture their hearts and souls with an *Inspiring Purpose*. As a leader, it is your job to communicate purpose and inspiration that pulls people together and forward. In Abraham Maslow's hierarchy, once basic needs (like food, safety, and belonging) are met, individuals seek self-actualization, which is the fulfillment of their potential and finding meaning in life. Purpose in work taps into this higher level of the hierarchy, providing people with the motivation to go beyond mere survival, just seeing their work as a means to earn a living and instead strive for personal growth and contribution.

People are more willing to exert effort when they believe their work has deeper meaning and contributes to their sense of purpose or self-fulfillment.

When you have *Great People* and they are aligned around and driven by an *Inspiring Purpose*, you must provide them with *Optimized Playbooks* so that they not only know what to do in their role but also so they can see how other team members are running plays around them. If you've ever watched a great orchestra perform, part of what makes the performance great is that all of the musicians are in perfect sync, and they are working off of the same composition. That is their playbook. Imagine if you brought together an orchestra, and the conductor told them what piece he or she wanted them to perform but didn't give them a composition to follow. It would likely be a cacophony of noise that would send you running from the theater. The magic happens when the orchestra is filled with great musicians who are inspired by the purpose of their performance, and they are each executing their playbooks—their compositions—to perfection.

You cannot *maintain* greatness without a *Culture of Performance*. The musicians in the orchestra have to practice. They have to receive feedback. They watch recordings of their performances and study their craft. Every professional performer and athlete has a practice schedule. They practice so that when it is time to perform, they know what to do and how to do it. Ironically, it is often the best of the best performers who practice the most.

Only in the world of business do we have professionals who don't value and invest in training and practice.

Your meetings, your Scorecards and Scoreboards, your onboarding and continuous training systems, those are where you practice. Legendary American football coach Vince Lombardi is widely attributed as the originator of the famous quote, "Practice doesn't make perfect. Perfect practice makes perfect." Lombardi emphasized the importance of practicing correctly, not just repeatedly, to achieve excellence. His philosophy was that only disciplined, focused, and precise practice could lead to mastery and true success.

Think about that statement and then look internally. Do people show up to your meetings on time and prepared, like an elite athlete showing up for practice? When your Scorecards and Scoreboards are off track, do you really attack the issues and exhaust every effort to get back on track? Do you take your projects and commitments to each other seriously and follow through for each other? Are you intentional and disciplined about your onboarding and training systems? You have to be willing to do things to a high standard all of the time if you are going to become an elite organization.

Finally, to pull it all together and ensure you maintain and grow the resources necessary to invest in extraordinary execution of the first four obsessions, you must maintain a disciplined focus on consistently *Growing Profits and Cash Flow.* Profits and cash are the fuel you put in the engine that is your business, and the more fuel you have, the further and faster you can accelerate toward fulfilling your *Inspiring Purpose.* The more fuel you can invest in the best talent and benefits, the best tools and software, the best facilities, and the best marketing strategies. No profit, no purpose.

When you get it right, you will begin to experience the concept of coherence, where the whole of your efforts and focus is far greater than the sum of its parts. That is when you will begin to earn not just a meaningful Return on Investment but a meaningful Return on Life… the Holy Grail we all seek during the finite amount of time we have on this earth.

PARTING THOUGHTS

Congratulations on taking this first step of discovery into making a meaningful investment in a bigger, bolder future by joining an outstanding group of organizations and leaders from across the country on a relentless journey to become their absolute best and to build truly elite organizations.

At the start of this book, I asked you to write down a date two years from the day you started reading it. I asked you to imagine your organization in two short years with all of the tools and systems in place to execute these *Five Obsessions* to a very high standard. Go back and reread that opening section of Chapter 1 and let yourself reground in that vision.

Really...try it and then come back to this page.

Can you see it in your mind's eye? Now that you understand the details, how much more valuable would it be for you, in two short years, to be joyfully on your way to that destination?

If you're the founder, or an owner, how much more would your business be worth in terms of real value in the marketplace? How much could you grow revenue and profit? How much would that improve the multiple that the business would be worth? On average, our clients grow their estimated Enterprise Value by 5.9 times, or 490 percent, in their first five years working with one of our Partners and Business Guides. That is a Return on Investment you likely cannot get anywhere else.

Do the math for yourself. What was your profit last year, and what is a conservative multiple that you believe your business is worth right now? Multiply that by 5.9 to see how much value you could create over the next five years. Keep in mind this is just the average. The best of the best teams and organizations do much, much better than that. If you estimate your business is worth five million dollars today, that may not be enough money to outlive you should you sell for that. If, however, you just performed to the average of our clients in this case study, you could expect to have a business worth roughly thirty million dollars in as little as five years. If your business is worth twenty million dollars today, performing to the average would mean your business could be worth over one-hundred million in just five years.

Even if you have no desire to sell, you will have an exit one way or another. The death rate is holding steady at 100 percent, so even if your business is passed down, you will exit. How much more bulletproof and sustainable will your business be if you are running it on the Five Obsessions? How much easier will it be for future generations if you lay the foundation and do the hard work now?

Make no mistake, if you decide to embark on this journey, it will not be an easy one. You will experience failures and defeats along the way. There will be disappointments, and people will let you down. Be glad for it. Every failure, every disappointment, and every setback is an opportunity to learn and grow. The journey is not about how many times you fail; it is about your commitment to excellence and your commitment to stay in the game, getting better and better on your relentless journey to build something elite.

In our experience, the most successful teams and organizations are the ones who push, challenge, and inspire each other to greatness. At the same time, they are also the ones who support each other, have each other's backs, and stick together when times get tough. They do this without ever losing focus on the Five Obsessions of Elite Organizations.

A GUIDED PATH TO AN ELITE ORGANIZATION

> "[The best advice I ever received was]
> to have a coach.... Every famous athlete, every
> famous performer has somebody who's a coach—
> somebody who can watch what they're
> doing and...give them perspective."[37]
>
> —ERIC SCHMIDT, Former CEO of Google

While this book was intentionally written to give you the ability to do it yourself, I would challenge you to consider three things before you start:

- Your time
- Your priorities
- Your proficiency

Your Time

When you consider the lift required to implement and customize everything you will need to get started and the effort that it will take to roll everything out to all levels of the organization, will you honestly be able to give this the time it needs and do it to the high standard being elite requires? I'm confident that you are completely capable. That is not the question.

Will you have the time to teach every leader and every team in your organization the tools? Will you have the time to drive accountability while maintaining your day-to-day responsibilities?

---

37 Eric Schmidt, "Bill Gates on Mentors," Every Bill Gates Video, October 13, 2015, YouTube video, 1:25, https://www.youtube.com/watch?v=ar2VNgRDGJ0.

Let me ask it another way: Is taking a do-it-yourself approach really the best use of your time, especially when you consider what your time is worth, including the opportunity cost of you trying to self-implement this principled approach instead of doing other things that are a higher and greater use of your unique value and time?

If not, this will take years, if not decades, to get done…and the odds are, you will start and quit because you will not be able to stay focused and give it the time and attention it requires.

Your Priorities

Think about your current priorities. Think about what you need to prioritize over the next few years. Can you create the space for self-implementation of the Five Obsessions to be your number one priority for the next two years? Can you avoid the temptation and pull of all the distractions to keep this alive and moving forward?

How have you done in the past with staying focused on your priorities and commitments? If you add this to your plate, how will you do?

If you cannot commit to keeping your focus on the Five Obsessions as your top priority, you will fail. There will be starts and stops, and your people will not follow you if you are not consistent. It is the *Law of the Lid*.[38] No one in the organization will rise to a level greater than the level to which they see you as their leader. If you are not consistent and focused on it, they will not be either.

---

38 John C. Maxwell, *The 21 Irrefutable Laws of Leadership: Follow Them and People Will Follow You* (Thomas Nelson, 1998).

Your Proficiency

Are you the right "who" to take this on? Do you have the experience and the passionate desire to be a teacher, facilitator, and accountability coach? Do you have the reps, or do you just dabble at things like this? When you consider the potential gains and long-term value of getting it right, does it make sense to do it yourself, or should you bring in an expert?

If someone you loved needed surgery, would you read books, study videos, and do it yourself? Of course not. You would research the best of the best surgeons and spare no expense to get your loved one in the most capable hands possible.

Our Next Level Growth Partners and Business Guides are the best of the best. We are all former owners, CEOs, or Presidents of businesses with more than ten million in revenue and fifty or more employees. We understand the complexities of leading businesses at scale, and we are obsessed with being elite at what we do. We collaborate regularly, sharing experiences, best practices, and lessons learned on the journey. Our clients benefit from our collaboration and experience shares. All of it is a result of our extreme passion to help YOU achieve greatness.

> "Alone we can do so little; together we can
> do so much. Having a guide transforms
> our potential into progress."[39]
>
> —HELEN KELLER

We hope that you will choose to put your faith in a Next Level Growth Partner to be your Guide on this journey. We have already helped hundreds of organizations who came before you. Many of them have

---

39 Helen Keller, *The Story of My Life* (Doubleday, Page, 1903).

already reached their Summits, and most of them made it up the mountain faster than they expected and are now on to a new, even bigger and bolder Summit. Some of them were as small as just a few million dollars in revenue when they started, and others were in the hundreds of millions when they roped in with us. It's not where you start; it's where you finish.

> *If you want to go fast, go alone.*
> *If you want to go far, go together.*
> *If you want to go fast and far,*
> *go with a Guide.*

The best views come after the hardest climbs. You may be just one conversation and one simple decision away from the one thing that will change everything for the better and help you take your business, and your life, to the Next Level. I'm inviting you to rope in with us, but you have to make the choice. You can either stick with the status quo, or be decisive and take ownership of a bigger, bolder future.

Let's climb!

Michael Erath

> If you enjoyed this book, please leave an Amazon review
> and share the book with your colleagues.

ADDITIONAL RESOURCES AND NEXT STEPS

- To take our Elite Organizations Assessment to see how you're doing in each of the Five Obsessions and get insights and guidance on how to take your organization, and your life, to the next level, visit **FiveObsessions.com/Assessment**
- To learn more about working with a Next Level Growth Partner and Business Guide, visit **NextLevelGrowth.com** and click the button to **"start a conversation"**
- To download resources from this book, visit **FiveObsessions.com**
- To keep up with our latest content, subscribe to our YouTube channel at **YouTube.com/@NextLevelGrowth**
- For a list of books we recommend for entrepreneurs and leaders, grouped by theme, visit **NextLevelGrowth.com/Recommended-Reading**
- Follow us on LinkedIn at **LinkedIn.com/company/NextLevelGrowthAZ**
- For an ever evolving and expanding list of available resources to help you on your journey, visit **NextLevelGrowth.com** and choose from the links in our menu such as **Workshops** and **Resources**
- To subscribe to and interact with my clone, where you can go even deeper on any of the Five Obsessions or get additional help with any of the tools and concepts from the book, visit **AskMichaelErath.com**

ACKNOWLEDGMENTS

This book would not have been possible without the people who accompanied me on this journey, and I cannot thank them enough for their impact on my growth.

Elizabeth, my encouraging and beautiful wife, thank you for your love, support, and encouragement throughout all the ups and downs of our decades together. I am truly a blessed man to have had you in my life since we were kids.

Matthew and Zachary, our boys, thank you for the joy you have brought to your mother and me along the way. Watching you grow into the fine young men that you are has been an extraordinary experience.

To my amazing parents, Shirley and the late George Erath. You have taught me so much and showed me so much of the world. I would never have achieved what I have without your love, support, and guidance.

To Cameron Herold for lighting a fire in me when you told me I was more than just an EOS Implementer and encouraged me to create my own thing.

To Scott Elser and Chris Prenovost, my friends, and the first Partners and Business Guides to join me at Next Level Growth when I decided to build a firm in 2019. Thank you for trusting me and both sharing and helping shape my vision. Your friendship and partnership have been invaluable.

To Greg Cleary and Duane Marshall, my fellow disruptors. Having a tribe on the journey we've been on together has been invaluable, and creating with you has been an outstanding experience.

Dr. Nido Qubein, thank you for your long-time family friendship and for the gift of your time in helping me with this book. What you have accomplished in my hometown has indeed been an *Extraordinary Transformation*. I am grateful for our conversations and the insights you have shared with me.

To Tanya Gagnon of Miss Details Design, for being able to see my creative vision and bring it to life in ways I never could.

Thank you also to my YPO and EO Forum mates over the years for your friendships, your honesty, and your help, making me a better version of myself.

Lauren Bailey, I am grateful for the awesome person that you are and for roping me in with you and your team. I appreciate you allowing me to be a part of your story and sharing an important piece of it in this book.

Brad Cox, congratulations on the outstanding accomplishments you and your family have achieved in not only maintaining but also growing a hundred-year-old family business through three generations, and now also making the investment to further strengthen the organization to be ready for the fourth generation. Thank you for allowing me to share your story.

David Miller and Jack Miller, for being the exceptional leaders that you are and for the culture you have helped build and curate at the Fairmont Scottsdale Princess. It brings a sense of joy and peace to Elizabeth and me to hear the stories that Zachary shares with us about how much he loves the organization and the people he works with and for. Creating what you and the rest of the leadership have is a rare and precious thing. Thank you for allowing me to share our son's story of his experience at the Fairmont Scottsdale Princess with our readers.

Thank you to the following test readers who gave their time and insights to help make this book what it is: Scott Elser, Chris Prenovost, Chris Roth, and Wendy Evans.

To all of the entrepreneurs and organizations that have put their faith in Next Level Growth, I cannot thank you enough. It is through our work with you and your teams that we are able to fulfill our purpose. You are the brave and courageous souls who are willing to do the difficult things and to make the hard decisions on a relentless journey to build something elite and take your business, and your life, to the Next Level. This book is a by-product of all of our work together.

We are honored to be roped in together and part of your journey.

BIBLIOGRAPHY

Covey, Stephen R., A. Roger Merrill, and Rebecca R. Merrill. *First Things First*. Free Press, 1994.

Deming, W. Edwards. *The New Economics: For Industry, Government, Education*. MIT Press, 1994.

Gerber, Michael. *The E-Myth Revisited: Why Most Small Businesses Don't Work and What to Do About It*. Harper Business, 1995.

Herold, Cameron. *Meetings Suck: Turning One of the Most Loathed Elements of Business into One of the Most Valuable*. Lioncrest Publishing, 2016.

Porter, Michael. *Competitive Advantage: Creating and Sustaining Superior Performance*. The Free Press, 1985.

Rock, David. *Your Brain at Work: Strategies for Overcoming Distraction, Regaining Focus, and Working Smarter All Day Long*. Harper Business, 2009.

Shelley, Mary. *Frankenstein*. New York, 1818.

Sinek, Simon. *Start with Why: How Great Leaders Inspire Everyone to Take Action*. Portfolio/Penguin, 2009.

Tuckman, Bruce. "Developmental Sequence in Small Groups." *Psychological Bulletin* 63, no. 6 (1965): 384–99. https://psycnet.apa.org/doi/10.1037/h0022100.

Willink, Jocko. "#197—Jocko Willink: War, Leadership, and Discipline." July 4, 2021, in *Lex Fridman Podcast*, 2 hours, 3 minutes. https://podcasts.apple .com/us/podcast/197-jocko-willink-war-leadership-and-discipline/id1434 243584?i=1000527824424.

ABOUT THE AUTHOR

MICHAEL ERATH is the founder of Next Level Growth, a firm of elite business guides with clients across the country who are committed to Helping Entrepreneurial Leaders Build Elite Organizations® while earning more than just a Return on Investment, but also a meaningful Return on Life. Next Level Growth works with entrepreneurs and their leadership teams to strengthen The Five Obsessions of Elite Organizations® utilizing a custom-tailored and principled approach to help each individual company reach its ultimate goals.

Michael has been a lifelong entrepreneur with twenty years of his career spent in the hardwood manufacturing industry, where his companies had offices on six continents around the world. He is also a former member of the Young Presidents' Organization's (YPO) Southern Seven Chapter and the Entrepreneurs' Organization's (EO) Columbus and Arizona Chapters, as well as a former record-holding EOS Implementer® and former Scaling Up Coach. During that time, Michael discovered a passion for helping entrepreneurs develop customized solutions for systemizing and scaling their businesses, which led to his transition to working as a business guide and to the founding of Next Level Growth.

Michael and his wife, Elizabeth, reside in Phoenix, Arizona. To learn more, or to reach Michael or a Next Level Growth Partner and Business Guide, visit NextLevelGrowth.com.

www.ingramcontent.com/pod-product-compliance
Lightning Source LLC
Chambersburg PA
CBHW030459210326
41597CB00013B/731